THE BEVERLY HILLS LECTURES
ON SPIRITUAL SCIENCE

THE
BEVERLY HILLS LECTURES
ON
SPIRITUAL SCIENCE

ERNEST HOLMES

Science of **Mind**
D E V O R S S

ISBN: 0-87516-702-0
Library of Congress Card Catalogue Number:
96-71714

Editor: Arthur Vergara
Contributing editor: Sandra Sarr
Cover design by Gary Peattie and Randall Friesen

Printed in the United States of America

DeVorss & Company, Publishers
Box 550
Marina del Rey, CA 90294-0550

Science of Mind Publishing
United Church of Religious Science
3251 West Sixth Street
Los Angeles, California 90020

Contents

THE BEVERLY HILLS LECTURES
ON SPIRITUAL SCIENCE

Introduction

NOWHERE ELSE in his other lecture series or writings do we find so much diversity of subject and such personally revealing history as in the talks that Ernest Holmes gave to an audience assembled at Beverly Hills High School on six consecutive Wednesday evenings in January and February 1952.

Although himself an ordained minister and the founder of a movement that today boasts hundreds of churches, Ernest Holmes never had a church of his own. Dr. Holmes preferred the nonreligious setting of lecture rooms and theaters to churches for his own speaking engagements, which his long-time associate Reginald Armor tells us he referred to as "our Sunday morning conferences."

For example, in the second lecture, Dr. Holmes not only addresses the presumed interest of his audience in psychology but draws upon his own decades of interest in the subject and its relevance to a *full* science of the mind. The valid scope and uses of psychology were in fact basic to his own understanding of the Science of Mind, which he early in his textbook of the same name refers to as "the science of Spiritual Psychology"; and later on he says, "Psychology and metaphysics are but two ends of the same thing."*

*SOM 27:4; 100:1.

Three other lectures—on metaphysics, healing, and spiritual mind treatment—not only take the reader into more personal reflections than we may find in Dr. Holmes' books, but in fact postdate his last works on these subjects by several years. By then in the last decade of his productive life, he had ever new things to say—solidly based, however, on the same science he first enunciated in print thirty-three years earlier in his *Creative Mind* and *Creative Mind and Success*.

One of the several differences between Dr. Holmes' books and his talks*—these latter always unscripted and unrehearsed—consists in the elevated level of stimulation and even of challenge the talks pose to his audience. Especially in his talks, Dr. Holmes' thought moves swiftly and in wide compass. Dr. Carol Hatch, who was long a mainstay at Founder's Church of Religious Science in Los Angeles, and who attended these lectures, once asked Dr. William Hornaday, Founder's pastor—also present on each of the six evenings—whether he understood everything that Dr. Holmes had said. *"Are you kidding?"* he replied.

Thus from complex ideas to deceptively simple observations, these pages extend an invitation to a journey of mind and spirit that few books in this field can equal. To draw closer to Ernest Holmes and to enter more profoundly into his thought are the treat and privilege that await each reader.

*Examples of printed talks include *Ernest Holmes Seminar Lectures* and the three volumes of *The Holmes Papers* series: *The Philosophy of Ernest Holmes*; *The Anatomy of Healing Prayer*; and *Ideas of Power*.

NOTE Dr. Holmes occasionally uses the generic *he* in pronoun references to both sexes—a common practice in his day. His usage implies no sexism, and its appearance can always be mentally translated into "he or she," "him or her," etc., as fits the case.

1

"YOU CAME FROM WHERE YOU ARE GOING TO"
THE METAPHYSICAL FRAMEWORK

I BELIEVE the world is on the verge of a great spiritual revival. The age of materialism passed out of science 25 years ago, and the age of spiritual realization is about to dawn upon us.

When science finally discovered that this thing which was called a material universe slivers away into a limbo of energy and invisible action, propelled by some form of intelligence with purpose and decision, the way was open for the writing of such a book as Compton's* *Freedom of Man*. Written ten years ago, it says that the materialist no longer has any right to talk as though he were giving us any spiritual values, because the new concept of the physical universe completely obliterates the materialistic hypothesis of something coming out of nothing. Jeans† wrote that we can think of the universe in terms

---

*Arthur H. Compton (1892–1962), American physicist and Nobel laureate.
†Sir James Jeans (1877–1946), English physicist, astronomer, and author.

of an infinite thinker, thinking mathematically; Edding-
ton, that all the laws of the universe act as though they
were intelligence moving as law. Men like Carrel* tell us
that faith acts as a law.

It is time, then, for us to realize that the world is ready
for a simple presentation of a metaphysical hypothesis,
a theory of practice, and a technique for using it. For the
last 75 to a hundred years, a religious and spiritual revo-
lution has been taking place in the human race. We are
one of the liberal branches of the new metaphysical
movement. We have a simple presentation that is consistent with all the great thoughts of the ages. There is nothing we shall discuss in these six evenings that does not
have a background in all of the major spiritual philosophies and religions of antiquity—medieval mysticism,
Grecian philosophy, and Jewish philosophy.

All of the facts are consistent with the great spiritual
teachings of the ages, starting with the Upanishads and
the Vedas, our own Bible, the medieval mystics, and the
modern metaphysical movement. These thoughts will not
necessarily be in line with the *theologies* of the ages, because, as Emerson† said, theology is the mumps, the
measles, and the whooping cough of the soul. The philosophy of a religion as it takes the form of a theology is
the things that happen to the intellect when the intuition
takes it along to the place where it bumps into cosmic
realities and causes reverberations in it and in the emotions, as well as a psychological and intellectual response
at the level of a person's culture and ability to think.

---

*Alexis Carrel (1873–1944), French surgeon, biologist, and Nobel
laureate.
†Ralph Waldo Emerson (1803–1882), American essayist and poet.

That is where we get all our religions. There is no other place they could come from. They are all intuitions, and they are all fundamentally and primarily right. When intuition strikes our intellect and emotion, it must interpret itself pretty much in our habitual thought-patterns. That is why we need not be too much concerned with the theologies. We would be lucky if our *own* were 50 percent right!

But we are concerned with the great spiritual intuitions and deductions and perceptions of the ages. Every advent in modern science marks a new inductive approach. Pythagoras* said that everything is motion and number. Now movement is in line with the forward thought of the world. I have watched it now for 40 years.† The things that Dr. Rhine‡ is now proving at Duke University, I was teaching years ago. Many of my friends said then, "You had better say that only in your classes, because it is pretty screwy stuff." I said, "Just give it time."

We have the possibility of doing something that has never been done in the world before—that is, providing a great object lesson of what can be done by any group of intelligent people who are dedicated to an idea, who

---

*(ca.580–ca.500 B.C.), Greek philosopher and mathematician.
†Holmes had first come to Los Angeles 40 years earlier (1912). James Reid, in "The First Religious Scientist," tells us: "He found Los Angeles an exciting place: a growing city of progressive people, in a ferment of expanding their horizons, not only physically, but mentally and spiritually. It was a community of stimulating intellectuals. Anything anyone might want to study was taught there. He said, many years later: 'I began to read and study everything I could get hold of.'"
‡Joseph B. Rhine (1895–1980), American psychologist and founder/director of the Institute of Parapsychology, Durham, N.C.

believe in it, understand it, feel it emotionally, and have an inward faith and conviction about it which makes it a reality to them. I consider that we are dealing with ultimate reality so far as we understand it—the most potential and potent force in the Universe. Whether we realize it or not, it has only been the few inspired leaders who have led the evolution of humanity throughout the ages. As Emerson said, "Our institutions are but lengthened shadows of their lives and teachings."

It is necessary in our movement that we have as many people as possible who will work with us and for us, knowing what they do, why they do it, and how to do it—and then *doing* it! We are part of a social order. We are part of an evolutionary epoch in the unfoldment of the human race, an evolutionary emergence of the push, or whatever you want to call this Thing-back-of-things which always shoves itself through an instrument that is prepared to receive it.

Always, when the time comes that humanity is ready for a new and greater concept of God, this evolutionary push uses it as an instrument to promote and carry forward the idea. This is the way humanity evolves. It does not evolve through the workings of the sum total of thinkers, but through the operation of a *few* of its *leading* thinkers. Take men like Buddha, Plato, Jesus, Socrates, Aristotle, and some 15 or 20 others away from human history, and we would not be as advanced as we are.

I believe our Institute* is one of the new emergents. I have believed it for 25 years. We are fortunate in our rela-

*The Institute of Religious Science, founded in Los Angeles in 1927.

tionships with those who work with us. There is a great
spirit of cooperation and unity, and a growing intelligence. I believe now that our movement has reached a
place where it can shoot forward with great impetus. But
it must have vision to prepare its own way. When you
reach a certain place, nothing can supply that vision but
yourself.

The moment you step out of the ordinary ranks, the
moment that you step out of the procession that moves
endlessly down the aisle, you are in a spotlight of evolution. Your own choice has decided you, and you are no
longer going to think as others. You are no longer going
to lay your greatness at the feet of a person whom you
recognize to be great. The moment a person steps out of
the endless stream of humanity, he no longer goes by the
norm that was set by the mass mind. He is a leader. He
is a thinker. He is one who introduces new things into the
world. He is now, in my mind, one specially chosen by
Cosmic Intelligence for a definite purpose. But he has to
create the vision ahead of himself!

I have said many times that of all the frustrated people in the world, the frustrated metaphysician is the
worst—because he has asked for more, believed in more.
He knows there *is* more. If you and I know there is some
secret and silent operation in our own consciousness that
can produce good for us and we don't use it, we are like
a light that is under a bushel. We are dissatisfied, unhappy, because we know we are not living up to the highest levels of our own consciousness.

Our Institute is in this position. We have done a very
good job; now the time has come to do a much better
job. With the cooperation of all our workers, all of our

teachers, I want to see if we can have 500 to 1000 people who know *what* they are doing, *why* they are doing it—and will come and *do* it. In spite of all the books that have ever been written, all the philosophies and religions—all of which are good—the world has never yet brought together as many as a thousand people who know spiritual truths and who will think alike (without arguing) long enough to let something happen. Before I die I want to prove something I believe in, something which in a very small degree you and I have proven in our individual lives.

The biggest life is the one that includes the most. There is something about the givingness of the Spirit within us that increases the possibility of our own evolution. We can no longer say to people, "We are going to save your soul." It doesn't make sense. But we *can* say this: "The Universe itself awaits the acknowledgment of man." If you don't believe it, watch the evolution of science. No laws are created—merely *potentials* are created. Someone surrenders himself to the genius of the Universe, and the Universe flows into him. Genius is nothing less than the ability of the intellect, will, and emotion to surrender themselves to something greater than themselves.

All the great teachings of the ages, in presenting spiritual truths, have described the nature of the Life principle, which is God, as a circle—the only thing that has neither beginning nor end. In this it describes infinity. The ancients used to describe it as a snake in the form of a hoop—a snake with its tail in its mouth—because the serpent was the Life principle, like a seamless garment, a ring. They represented it as a three-headed serpent—the serpent of the earth, the air, and the sky—the Father, Son, and Holy Ghost as we have it today.

It was the serpent who talked to Eve and tempted her. In the allegory, Eve stands for the feminine, or what today we call the psyche or subjective part of us. It receives the suggestion, and when the suggestion has been assimilated, the object (or Adam) is said to have impregnated it. So we find that Moses lifted up the serpent in the wilderness on a cross. The cross stands for the Tree of Life— its head in the sky, its feet on the ground, its arms outstretched to shadow the earth. The ancients had an inverted tree, or cross, whose roots were in the sky, and which flowered on earth.*

All this represents the two great principles with which all the great systems of antiquity dealt.† You will find them in the opening chapters of Troward's‡ *Bible Mystery & Bible Meaning* and in the first chapters of my textbook.§ They aren't called that, because people are afraid of the terms. What it means is the descent of Spirit into matter. It is what Browning refers to when he says in one of his poems that "a spark disturbs our clod." In the order of the creative process, we have the descent of Spirit into matter, the divine spark reaching the lowest level of the evolutionary round of life, impregnating it, and asleep in it—"asleep" in the sense that in the process of evolution, it shall finally return to the Father's house.

This is the meaning of the Prodigal Son. An individualized creative center,‖ unified with the whole, must go

*See p. 102.
†I.e., the objective and subjective in the Cosmic (and individual) creative process.
‡Thomas Troward (1847–1916), English colonial administrator, jurist, and metaphysical writer.
§*The Science of Mind.*
‖I.e., the individual.

through the processes of evolution in self-discovery and never lose that one valuable thing—the whole cause and purpose of its creation—which lies in the innumerable individualizations of Cosmic force, rooted in unity, yet flowering into multiplicity. To quote Emerson, we find "unity at the center and multiplicity at the circumference"; "one mind common to all individual men." The ancients called it the Great Unconscious. I suppose in a similar sense the solar energy is caught in the atom. It has always been there, but it was never exploded until the evolutionary process perfected some intelligence that knew how to loose it.

The thing that is unique about Religious Science isn't that *we* have it. It was inevitable that *someone* would have it. *I* didn't make it up. It claims no originality but borrows from *every* originality, on the assumption that Truth is not a personal thing but belongs to the one who uses it. We have a right to take from every system that which is affirmative, that which makes it work, to put it into a synthesis and say, "This is the best the world has discovered. This is where we want to begin." That is the unique thing about Religious Science. I discovered many years ago that there was something I wanted to find out. *This is it.*

We start out with Spirit, Soul, and Body—or the Thing, the Way It Works, and What It Does (see the opening chapters of our textbook). This includes the masculine, active, self-conscious, impregnating, volitional aspect of the Universe—thinking, willing, knowing, doing through thought—and the feminine, which is psychologically the subconscious or what we call subjectivity (and we believe in *universal* subjectivity). It is as inevitable as the law of gravity that holds you in place here and that held King David in place when he wrote his lyrics.

Here is the masculine and feminine principle, the Adam and Eve in the individual. It is God moving upon the face of the deep, it is divine Mind impregnating the womb or soul of Nature. This is the medium for the operation of the Law of Cause and Effect. It is the principle of Mind. Mind or intelligence in a conscious state is the power that knows itself. The subconscious, subjective, and even the unconscious of Freud all mean the same thing. This is our psychosomatic relationship. Some day we shall get back to the original idea of the Greeks and the Jews who taught that man is spirit, soul, and body. Christianity is a combination of two ideas. I suggest that you read *Destiny of Western Man* by Dr. Stace* of Yale. He says that Christianity is the result of Jewish impositionalism and Grecian immanentism.

If you study your own nature, you find that you have a mind, although no one knows what it is. The mind is self-conscious. You know yourself. When you think, something happens. It goes into the subconscious, subjective, unconscious field, which seems to be a creative medium that affects conditions of the body. That is the theory of psychosomatic counseling, of psychosomatic medicine, or body-mind relationship. But remember: there is no body-mind relationship conceivable unless there is first a mind that observes and experiences the relationship.

The ancients taught, and we teach, that the Universe is Spirit, Soul, Body—conscious Intelligence, infinite

*Walter T. Stace, American academic and philosopher.

Presence. Yet you can't tell where the body leaves off and the mind begins. It is as Einstein says: energy is mass in fluid form, and mass is energy in a solid form. He has given us a great scientific approach to our own philosophy, because we say that the manifestation is the thing manifest *in the form of what it does*. We don't say that thought operates *on* an object; we say that thought operates *as* the object. Einstein doesn't say that energy energizes mass; he says energy *is* mass—that they are equal, identical, and interchangeable.*

If someone says it is all Mind in manifestation, that would be a philosophy consistent with Einstein's last equation. At any rate, here is the reason that God is the "I am"; and *I am* is a statement of the verb *to be*. Moses said that the word of life, the word of power, is in your own mouth. The ancient Upanishads, the Vedas, the Bhagavad Gita taught these things. These were the things that Gandhi studied.

"Lift the rock and you will find Me, cleave the rock and there am I." God is in everything and through everything, making everything what it is. We believe that, and every great thinker who ever lived believed it. There is nothing in modern psychology or modern science to dispute it. In fact, every new discovery tends to prove it right. This is your own nature—you are spirit, soul, and body; and there is something within you that is acted upon, as a result of which something happens to you.

In psychology it is believed that every individual has

---

*In fact, Dr. Holmes was looking beyond Einstein to the fundamentally holistic, organic concepts that quantum theory, which had few adherents in 1952, and which was not accepted by Einstein, would make a cliché in our own time.

a mind (a psyche) and a body. They believe that as a result of thoughts, certain things affect the body. They are wrong there.* If the mind I use is different from the mind you use, we could not recognize each other. It is only because there is one Mind common to all individuals that you know me and I know you. We say there is only one subjective Mind in the Universe and that what psychologists analyze as our psyche, or subjective mind, is merely our *place* in *a universal field* of Mind. You see, the psychologists say: "You have a subjective mind, and we will analyze it to find out what's wrong with you." Their facts are not coordinated.

In other words, suppose each one of us goes out into an unknown country and works an acre of land. There are 250 acres, and each one will take an acre in the same land. There are not 250 different kinds of creative processes in the soil; there is only *one* kind of creative process common to the 250 acres. But we are people; so each one plants his plot the way he likes it. Then everything is different when it comes up, and people who see it say, "Here are 250 individual acres of land."

There is no such thing! There are 250 *individualized plots* of *one creativity* operating through this soil. Now, that is exactly the way it is with "your" subjective mind and "mine." There is really no such thing as what the

---

*Dr. Holmes appears to have in mind the limitations of psychosomatics, with its predication of mind-body interaction, in which thought is supposed to operate *on* an object (see above), whereas "we say that thought operates *as* the object," just as "energy *is* mass . . . equal, identical, and interchangeable." This nondual state of things sets the context for what he next says about the "one Mind common to all individuals."

pyschologist calls "your" subjective mind. Each of these acres did have different kinds of plants; but there was only one "principle" in the soil that operated upon different "ideas" to produce them.

So every man, as a result of his thinking, subjectifies that thinking. It passes into what we call "his" subjective mind; but his subjective mind is really a universal creativity flowing through everything and now surrounding him with the reaction of his own thinking, which in its turn is reacting on its own environment. That is the principle of our philosophy. Both the conscious and the subconscious are *Mind*. Psychology says that the *individual psyche* is the *whole mind*, conscious and subconscious. We say that Mind—the Mind Principle, which is universal—is *individualized*.

The only thing that is conscious is the Spirit. The nearest we can arrive at it is through our conscious intelligence, with the possibility of its endless intuitive perceivings and its infinity of self-knowingness from which it draws its inspiration—because there are inverted roots up there, coming down to form the tree, or cross, here, and taking root here. This is the process of involution—taking root here to complete the cycle and return to the Father's house by an evolutionary push. Lloyd Douglas* says that the forces are equal because they are aligned. If they were not equal, the pressure from here could never emerge at the level of its own awareness.† Jesus understood it when he said, "It is done unto you *as* you believe." His "as"

---

*(1877–1951), American Congregational clergyman and novelist.
†"Return to the Father's house," "emerge at the level of its own awareness," etc.: metaphors for *demonstration* in mental science.

qualifies, and appears to limit, the Infinite in its capacity, because no matter how much it pours over us, only as much as our bucket will hold shall we retain at any given time.

So far as you and I are concerned, it means that there is some part of us—spirit, soul, psyche, subjective mind, reaction—and there is body,* where we individualize the Cosmic order. Jesus said, "First the Father works, and now the Son works." In all the teachings of the great mystics you will find this theory, that the Thing which impregnates everything, whether it be a human or a Cosmic atom, is God. The energy concealed in it is God, just as the energy concealed in the physical atom is soma.

Just as soon as the evolving entity arrives at the place where it turns from the clod and develops reflective consciousness, from that moment on its individual evolution ceases until it learns consciously to cooperate with Nature and Nature's laws. All evolution now is a partnership. The Father worketh until now—but now the Son works! The Father has inherent life within Himself, so He has given it to the Son to have inherent life within Himself— that whatsoever the Son seeth the Father do, that also may the Son do, that the Father may be glorified. That is what Jesus was talking about.

Human evolution arbitrarily stopped as a Cosmic mandate whenever that time was when people knew they were different from their environment. From then on, all the laws of Nature awaited our self-discovery. But there is always an urge here and a pull there, something pulling onward, something pushing onward and upward. As

---

*"The entire manifestation of Spirit" (SOM 577, s.v. "Body").

Jesus said, "Who hath seen me hath seen the Father." Philip said, "Show us the Father and it sufficeth us." Jesus answered, "Have I been so long with you and yet thou hast not known? Who hath seen me hath seen the Father. Believe I am in the Father, and the Father in me, or else believe me for the works' sake." In other words, "I have told you this is the way it is. I want to prove it to you because of what I am doing." And they asked, "By what authority can you forgive sins?" The only authority Jesus ever cited was *the proof that his principle was right** — and that is the only authority you and I are ever going to have.

Our movement will depend not on a talk such as I am giving you now. Our evolution—what it will mean to the world—will not depend on the books we write. It will depend on what we *do* with it. It will depend on someone knowing enough about it to cause something to happen *because of what he knows—when* he wants it to happen, *where* he wants it to happen, in the *way* it ought to happen, according to his own volition, proving that he is not subject to any whimsical caprice.

Dr. Rhine understood that when he undertook the investigation of psychic phenomena. He is saying this: throughout the ages people have heard things and seen things; but the thing we must realize is that all the philosophies in the world are not worth a nickel unless they will work. Every philosophy of optimism that does not operate is a frustration. Every religious conviction that does not bear witness to objective manifestation and inward sanctification is a frustration. All the complex inhibition and frustration is a lack of the intellectual, emo-

---

*I.e., by the demonstration of it.

tional, and objective, manifest fulfillment of something that the psyche knows to be within itself. We start *here*, and the whole impulse is to get back *here*—because by some divine inward awareness, man has never left himself without a witness. "Standeth God within the shadows, keeping watch upon His own." We are going forward in an endeavor of mind and spirit to see what relationships we may have with this Oversoul, this all-Soul, this Spirit which we call God.

Dr. Rhine writes of clairvoyance and clairaudience. He is a scientific man and he doesn't believe in anything supernatural. Everything is according to law and order in its own field. What is true on one plane is true on all. It is the meaning of Jacob's Ladder. Dr. Rhine said: I want to subject all these things to a psychological check—for if the universe is law and order, I shall finally discover how to be able to reproduce all these "psychic" things at will. From experience to experiment, he has already done most of them.

It is a terrific thing, because it robs our field of superstition and leaves it open to the conscious use of mentality: here are extended, extrasensory perceptions which we all have, but which we have related to something external to ourselves, not knowing that everything is *here* that is ever going to come out of *here*. You are a spirit now just as much as you are ever going to be. Whatever you are going to be able to know by and by, you are able to know *now*. That is his theory.

We make an investigation in a similar way and, in a sense, in a similar field. We say this: in every religious shrine in the world where people have been healed—Catholic, Protestant, Jewish, Mohammedan—at any altar where people have worshiped—"miracles" have been provided. Did God intervene? No. Intelligence will say there is something in Nature which responds. Jesus said, "It is done unto you *as* you believe." He knew that there is a Power greater than we are that operates upon our beliefs, operating on the Cosmic forces. All the different denominations—and they are all good, although not identical in their philosophic content—have these "miracles." It is the *belief* that does it. That is the secret. That is the thing to follow up.

There is something that operates on our thinking—and when I say our thinking, I mean on the whole body of our thoughts. We must believe in something that elevates our thoughts. Jesus said, "Seek ye first the kingdom of God." In other words, he recognized a coordinating will, a pattern, a universal integrity, a justice without judgment: there is no sin but a mistake, no punishment but a consequence.

I believe the laws of mind work just like the laws of physics. I believe the Universe is one system. I am not trying to materialize mind or spiritualize matter. God is One; the creative Power that projects everything is One. In what it projects it is still one, although it wears many faces. Browning said, "What entered into thee / That was, is, and shall be: / Time's wheel runs back or stops: / Potter and clay endure."

And so we say that the individual mind is merely an individualization of the Cosmic Mind. It is a certain process of evolution (not the Mind Principle—God does not evolve). You attach your belief to a bigger belief: this is identification of the individual with the Universal, or man with God. We consciously believe all the laws of Nature are universal laws operating automatically upon their formations. There is a universal Intelligence operating automatically upon the foundation of our own individualized psyche.

Jesus said, "No man has ascended up into heaven, except he who came down from heaven—even [namely] the Son of Man who is in heaven." All he is saying is that you came from where you are going to—and there is nowhere to go, because *you are already there!* John said, "Beloved, now are we the sons of God, and it doth not yet appear what we shall be, but we know that, when he shall appear, we shall be like him; for we shall see him as he is."

Now, what does that mean? Whatever this thing is that we're going to be, we must be like *now*. "Ye shall know the truth, and the truth shall make you free." That is what they were talking about. All right, then: it is all belief— and our belief is operated upon.

Let's recapitulate. Before I get through with this series of talks, you will see that without what I've said tonight, what we are going to talk about is impossible to understand. Without it, we are talking about higher mathematics without knowing how to add, subtract, divide, and multiply. We must know the mechanics and the spontaneous side of things. We've got to put the spirit and the letter together, the art and the artist, the creator and creation. So we have to start with a broad generalization, always remembering that for every specialization—for everything in the Universe that is manifest—there is a universal quality, element, form, Life, Mind, and Soul behind it that makes it what it is.

We must expect to find within ourselves (the microcosm, man) a miniature reproduction of the macrocosm (God). Einstein tells us that light, time, and space bend back upon themselves. He has probed the nature of the physical universe until he has discovered the laws. "As a man sows, so shall he reap." Everything that goes out comes back. We shall discover that energy and mass are equal, identical, and interchangeable. *So are thoughts and things.* You can theoretically reduce circumstances to a chain of mental reactions. But dissolve the causation, and you will dissolve the chain of effects.

There is something within us that cannot be satisfied until it finds an abiding-place in the only security there is—the Cosmos itself—without losing self. "For Thou hast made us; Thine we are; and our hearts are restless 'till we find repose in Thee."

2

<u>Wednesday 23 January 1952</u>

"SEE THROUGH
TO THE PERFECT FORM"
THE PSYCHOLOGY OF TOMORROW

IN INTRODUCING the subject of spiritual healing, I would like to say that, as it is practiced consciously as a science, a philosophy, and a spiritual concept throughout the world today—and particularly in America, where it originated—it is something entirely new in the world.

We speak of the Bible and indeed all the bibles and the ancient books of wisdom containing the philosophies which underlie this practice as taught by the great philosophers—Jesus, Emerson, Plato, etc. But until the advent of this new movement, which originated in the state of Maine a little over a hundred years ago,* nothing was known or written about what today interests from 15 to 20 million people in the United States.

It would be impossible to go back prior to that and hope to discover anything that had ever been written

---

*The reference is to the investigations and findings of Phineas Parkhurst Quimby (1802–1866).

which would even intimate that there is a science of Mind or a spiritual science, and that there is a technique for using it that actually works. It is a new science in the world. No one in this room initiated it. *I* certainly didn't. It is a new concept which probably explains the miracles of Jesus, the miracles at the religious shrines of the world. It explains—and gives the only adequate philosophy back of—modern psychology.

William James* said that the psychology of tomorrow will be metaphysics. That is inevitable, and he sensed it because he had spent years investigating spiritual things and psychic phenomena as well as psychology. He knew that the time will come when we shall know there is no such thing as the individual mind separate from the universal Mind, and no such thing as an individual person separate from the universal. We are all acted upon by Cosmic forces which are spiritual, by universal laws which are laws of cause and effect, and by universal forces which are the cause of everything. There must be a spiritual or invisible pattern in which all physical objects are rooted. So there is no use going into the evolution of spiritual philosophy throughout the ages. We must realize that we are dealing with something that has taken place in the last hundred years, the last 50 years, and more particularly the last 25 years.†

We want to study the sources of this new science, whether we call it Science of Mind, New Thought, Reli-

---

*(1842–1910), American psychologist and philosopher.
†100 years: P. P. Quimby. 50 years: by the turn of the century, major metaphysical organizations were in place (e.g. Divine Science, Unity, Home of Truth). 25 years: in 1927 Holmes founded the Institute of Religious Science.

gious Science, Divine Science, Unity, Church of Truth, or the science of metaphysics. They all teach the same thing; but they don't *believe* they teach the same thing. We are not interested in their differences of opinion; we are interested in what makes it work, because whatever makes it work is a universal Truth operative wherever it is perceived and used.

A little over a hundred years ago a man by the name of Phineas Quimby, a clock-maker who lived in the state of Maine, became interested in the experiments of Mesmer*—in mesmerism and hypnotism. He was a natural philosopher, a natural religionist, and a natural scientist —although at the time he was called a fool and a charlatan. His book† is probably among the dozen most original works of the human mind. It is a complete departure from anything that had ever been known before. It is quaint, but it contains most of the philosophy of the New Thought movement and all of the allied movements, and most of the methods now called spiritual mind healing— and most of what has been discovered in the field of psychology.

Quimby saw these experiments in mesmerism and thought he would try them out. He got a young man by the name of Lucius Burkmar, whom he could hypnotize easily. We know that hypnotism is the temporary abeyance of the objective faculties so that the subconscious, or whatever this inner field of mind is, comes to the surface. Quimby discovered that in the hypnotic state this boy could diagnose disease. He could tell what was going

---

*Franz Anton Mesmer (1734–1815), German physician.
†See *Phineas Parkhurst Quimby: The Complete Writings* (DeVorss).

on at a distance. He could prescribe remedies. For example, it was thought at the time that no one could be hypnotized if there was a thunderstorm. This came from Mesmer, who thought it had something to do with "animal" or electric magnetism in the human body. Quimby discovered that it made no difference. This was one of his first discoveries—realizing that he was dealing with a nonphysical force.

We must pass over all his experiments quickly, because he was about 25 years conducting them. When he passed away in 1866, he had probably healed more people than anyone who has ever been in this field. Whether he ever realized that he was dealing with a universal principle, I don't know.

During his experiments he developed what he called spiritual clairvoyance. I suppose he would have made a wonderful medium; but Quimby did not go along with the spiritualists or the theosophists.* This man was deeply religious and spiritual, but he was not superstitious. He wasn't afraid of anything or anybody, because he spoke from a native, inward perception of truth, which always transcends ordinary processes of reasoning and seems to speak from a more rounded, Cosmic realization of something which goes beyond the intellect, announces itself as using the intellect, and surrenders itself to it as an instrument for that which the intellect has identified itself with.

In all of his healings, Quimby used a spiritual power. This is the forerunner, the foundation, of all metaphysical spiritual mind healing. Each one has interpreted and restated his theory in a different way; but when you ana-

---

*Theosophists: i.e., their thought, either later or prototypical.

lyze it, it is the same thing. Quimby said that mind is matter in solution, and matter is mind in form. But he said that both of these things taken together are merely two sides of *one* thing, and the two of them constitute the "matter of Spirit." It is interesting that for the first time there has come out of the field of science another kind of explanation, in one of Einstein's theories. He said that energy and mass are equal, identical, and interchangeable. He doesn't say they are two different things. He says they are the same thing. But they have two forms: one is fluid, the other is temporarily solid. One you don't see and one you do see.

Quimby said that all disease is mind taking the objective form that corresponds to what today we would call its subjective or unconscious image. But, he said, back of both of these there is a wisdom, a Spirit, a divine Intelligence, a God—and a *spiritual* man. Mind as fluid, and matter as its form, constitute a dual unity, which in itself constitutes the "matter of Spirit." This is the basis of psychosomatic medicine, and that will probably eventually accept the whole metaphysical concept.

Having come to these conclusions, Quimby began to make experiments. He made up his mind that all physical disease is a malformation attaching itself to a spiritual image. It is a shadow, not a thing in itself. The Platonists had discovered the same thing, but they didn't name it. Quimby made up his mind that disease is some kind of image of mind, a thought held until it appears in the body, but that it is a mental phenomenon. He didn't say that disease is unreal. He said it is a logical result of the movement of mind upon itself, creating a form like itself,*

*I.e., like its "image."

which we experience. This is important to us, because it explains the method used by every school of New Thought in the world today.

Quimby concluded that if matter is mind in form, and mind is matter in solution, and if there is a superior wisdom which manipulates both, then both are subject to a higher wisdom. He said that Jesus had access to this wisdom. You will find this in his manuscripts in a large section called "Christ or Science."* Then he evolved the idea that if this is true, he might heal his own kidney trouble. He hypnotized Lucius and succeeded in healing his own condition.

Considering his own cure, he concluded that it was a natural thing: whatever was transpiring was in accord with the laws of Nature. It could be reduced to a science; it could be taught, practiced, and made to produce results. He insisted that all disease is mental in its origin. He didn't deny the body, he didn't say people were not sick; but he said the causation is mental. And he said it would have to follow that if disease is mind in form, then in some way that we don't understand, it is projected by mind and is itself a form of mind. It is a thought form, and consequently an opposite thought form should neutralize it. So he began to experiment along those lines.

He would say, This thing is a thought form, projected by our ignorance, our fear or superstition. It isn't normal

---

*Dr. Holmes was wont to point out three sections of *The Quimby Manuscripts* as yielding "the modern metaphysical movements." These are "Questions & Answers," "Christ or Science," and "The World of the Senses" (none of these titles original with Quimby). See *The Complete Writings of P. P. Quimby*, vol. 2, pp. 376, 377, and vol. 3 *passim* for these writings.

to be sick, it isn't natural, it isn't right. There is something that can heal him.

He starts his argument by saying that God is all there is, there is one Life, that Life is God, that Life is perfect. He goes on to deny everything that appears to contradict that perfection and to affirm everything that affirms it. He will explain and explain and explain until there isn't a shred of evidence in the logic of human reasoning to support the fallacy of this person's disease.

He began to experiment, and he began to get results. People came to him from all over the country. He said, It isn't an answer to prayer when I heal someone. *It is a spiritual science*, which Jesus understood.

I want to link this up with something else. Quimby supposed that back of all manifestation there is a pattern, a perfection which you and I did not make. All great thinkers have believed it. Quimby found that during the process of his explanation, people were healed. He found that they could be somewhere else and they would be healed. He discovered that the method was just the same whether the person was absent or present.

Dr. Rhine has discovered that you can plant grass or grain and affect it by blessing one part and cursing the other. His next experiment is to have people 500 miles away do the blessing and cursing. They will get the same results, because there is no distance. At Stanford University, they have had an endowment for many years to investigate psychic phenomena, and it is my understanding that they have a whole "museum" of reports under lock and key which they don't dare release.

So Quimby said, I'll argue this one down. He found that he could, and he did. He said, "You ask me what is my cure, and my answer is: my explanation is my cure."

There are only two methods used today: one is called the *argumentative* method, the other the *realization*. Man emerges from something; he comes from an invisible source into the visible. Quimby supposed that man is perfect—because God is a universal Principle, Presence, and Mind; and man is part of this Principle. And so he said, We'll trace man back to his original source. We shall find that he is perfect in God. He is part of the universal Principle. If there is anything wrong with him, it is something that has been attached.

Disease is not a thing in itself. In psychology, diseases have come to be called *compromises* we make with life— unconscious compromises, or the result of the effect of them. Quimby said, I'll go back to where man is perfect. There is but one Mind, one Intelligence, one Substance. What you see and what you don't see is the Substance that appears and disappears. What controls it is a superior wisdom. I represent that superior wisdom. He said that, often while sitting by his patient, he could see through to the perfect form. We are aware that there is a spiritual Presence, a spiritual identity, a spiritual entity —a Reality. It doesn't matter what you call it.

Now let's forget Quimby for a while, because I want to show you something else that will eventually lead to similar conclusions in the field of psychology. In modern psychology, 40 years after Quimby, and more particularly in the last 25 years, ideas began to evolve from Freud and others before him. Psychologists postulated what they called the *id* and the *libido*. The id means the "It"—the true unconscious, which to the psychologist means the true *unknown*. There is something from which everything emerges and, as it emerges in the individual's stream of consciousness, it is what is called the libido. The libido is defined as the emotional craving for self-expression within all things, the repression of which leads to psychoneurosis.

The theory is that back in infancy, born out of the unknown id, there is an emotional necessity for self-expression. That's why artists paint and singers sing, why a child makes mud pies—the need to create and to project. Then they decided that there are certain laws of the libido, the first being that it must have an object. This is important. *The libido must love something.* It must have the gratification of loving something or someone. And the love must not be rejected. These two laws are fundamental to every neurosis, every psychosis, every inward conflict, every emotional maladjustment. These are the common denominators running through all the fields of the new psychology. The libido must have an object; the libido must not be rejected.

What happens if the libido does not have an object and is rejected? Remember, here's a psychic stream of Cosmic energy individualizing itself. We speak of action and reaction, cause and effect, and we're right; but how often do we key the sequence of events back to the Thing that acts, that produced the action that produced the reaction? The sequence of the creative cause with us starts with absolute Intelligence, then the word, then the Law, and then the thing. That's the sequence of the creative order. It has to be.

There's a stream of Cosmic, psychic, and spiritual energy emanating from the universal Source which we call God, now individualizing in a person as an object for its own infinite libido. Not that I think it would hurt God's feelings if we rejected Him; but it short-circuits the Cosmic movement in us, until finally we make such readjustments as permit the circuit to resume its natural course. When that happens, we are automatically acted upon by the original Cosmic force that created us, knows all about it, and in a sense awaits the redemption of our own surrender, not to a higher will or a greater power, but to a more complete manifestation of That which is the essence of will and the action of power.

Freud and the earlier analysts discovered that when the libido is rejected, the ego not wanted, the energy flows back on itself. Freud said that all repressions are the result of highly emotionally charged thoughts and ideas—feelings so deeply repressed in what he called the unconscious that they cannot be brought to the surface either by an act of will or through the imagination. Those are his exact words.

Now, that's quite a thing, because a repression is not something that you know is there. If you knew it was there, the very knowing would make it lose its psychic energy, and it would flow out naturally. Therefore we have the modern theory known as psychoanalysis, causing the patient to release all these tensions through the careful manipulation of the analysis until all the forgotten memories come to the surface. I'm not attempting to explain psychology to you, but it's something I'll take a few moments to go into later.

Karen Horney,* founder of the American Institute for Psychoanalysis, wrote such books as *Our Inner Conflicts*

*(1885–1952), American psychoanalyst.

and *Neurosis and Human Growth*. She says that at the core of every neurosis you will find four things: a sense of rejection, a sense of guilt, a sense of insecurity, and a sense of anxiety. That's the sequence, the order of the conflict. Sometimes one or two are more dominating than the others.

The conflict itself is what takes place in the id (the Cosmic stream) pressing for fulfillment. It creates a disturbance, a conflict, because the sense of rejection is always pushing it back and the Cosmic urge is always pushing it forward. This is the nature of the inner conflict—what takes place when they talk of resolving the conflict, getting it out, clearing the passage. In this process some interesting things happen that I'd like to mention to you.

We're really setting the basis for a general, very broad outline for what's back of psychological and metaphysical healing as we understand it. It isn't adequate, it isn't complete, it isn't the last word—but it's all we have been able to put together.

When we are born out of this Thing psychologists call the id, or the God of the Cosmos, we're born for the purpose of individualizing and reproducing the Cosmos on a miniature scale. That's the purpose of existence, so far as anyone can figure out. Therefore, it is only as we live creatively that we live happily. There is nothing beyond happiness. All people who are overly aggressive whistle to keep up their courage, because psychologists tell us that aggression is the covering up of an inward sense of insecurity, inadequacy, and insufficiency. All power, all wealth, all everything that the human mind holds worthwhile is worthless without happiness.

Since the first object of the evolving libido of the infant

is its parents, its first emotional nature is attached to them. In its logical evolution it reaches a stage where it identifies itself with them. Then it reaches out to a place where it can be on its own. These are the normal stages. When an entity becomes itself and goes on to adulthood, it is self-expressed. Consequently Freud held that you have actually to get way back before you can get psychological clearance of the unconscious so that the original stream may flow to the outer end of objectivity. They discovered that in the process, all the things way back that inhibited the flow had to come to the surface and be self-seen. The original object of the libido must be temporarily restored in order that they may get the psychological reaction that the person in early youth, or in babyhood, originally had.

This "transference" is said to be either positive or negative according to the reactions the person had to his parents, whether he liked them or did not like them. We'll say the little boy hated his father and he goes to an analyst later in life. He might transfer his hate to the analyst. That would be a negative transference. It must be reduced to a positive one. Women transfer their love to the analyst, and it becomes a delicate thing to restore them, because the person isn't whole until he becomes whole within himself or herself. All healing is self-healing.

During this process another thing happens that interests me very much. Let's make it specific. Suppose the *analyst* hated *his* father and he were to come to the place in an analysis where he reaches the emotional reaction in the history of his patient where *he* also hated *his* father. The analyst will not be able to see, or understand, or go any further with the analysis. It's a block and remains a block until the analyst heals himself!

Jung,* who was the greatest of them all, said it doesn't make any difference what the analyst says to his patient; it is what he *thinks* that will register, not what he says. Jesus asked, How can the blind lead the blind? An analyst must not have any criticism of his patient, no condemnation. All of his criticism is an unconscious judgment of himself, whether he knows it or not. There wouldn't be this judgment of himself if his own channels were clear, the flow a complete thing.

It is known in psychology that this inner stream which comes out here and gets stopped creates a thing that is almost an entity. It may be a strange, crazy thing to say that every disease is a psychic† entity, but it is. There isn't any doubt about it. Joseph Jastrow‡ has said that one of the chief things the analyst has to contend with is what he calls the inertia of thought patterns. He said they argue as though they were entities. You remember when Jesus started to cast out the devils, they cried out, "Why do you torment us, son of David?"

Here is what in many fields of metaphysics they call the argument of error. Long before psychology worked it out, they called it the catharsis, which means the psychic purge. It discharges a substance from the subconscious; it's Carter's Little Liver Pills for the mind. Jung even speaks of psychic pus, as though he were comparing it with a sore spot, and of course that's exactly what Quimby did. You can change it and dissolve it by arguing it out of existence. There are sometimes multiple per-

---

*Carl Gustav Jung (1875–1961), Swiss psychologist and psychiatrist.
†I.e., of the psyche.
‡American psychologist and author.

sonalities in there, a dozen different kinds of complexes and conflicts, each one of which seems to be "itself."

I wanted to introduce this thinking because people in our field should know how close are the many things in other fields. If the world knew how close a synthesis of modern therapeutic psychology comes to our basic principle, they would at once see where our principle supplies that which that synthesis still lacks. It would automatically provide a philosophy for psychology which psychology has not reached out to as yet. Some day someone will make a complete synthesis of psychology and compare facts with facts, thought with thought, ideas with ideas, starting way back in the original id and just calling it the Cosmic urge, calling the libido the stream of Cosmic energy. This is what will happen.

Psychology, in a sense, individualizes Universality, and, in a very definite sense, in our field we universalize individuality. We find the place where they meet and merge, never separated, because it is the Universality coming to a point of individualization, or the Infinite becoming the finite. All of these laws will still obtain, but we will say the psyche is universal. We will call it Spirit; and we'll call the body the manifestation of Nature. The philosophy will be well rounded, its logic will justify its assumptions. Some day everyone who has a complete synthesis of what is known in psychology will walk into our field. He'll just put the thing together and say, with Pope,* "It's all a part of one stupendous Whole / Whose body Nature is, with God the soul." There's only one Spirit flowing into all people, taking the form of the

*Alexander Pope (1688–1744), English poet.

person it flows into. There is only one Mind, both conscious and subconscious. There can't be two, because there aren't two principles of Mind.

Read *The Philosophy of Plotinus*, by Inge.* It's difficult reading, but interesting. He says every organ of the body is attached to its own pattern, a divine pattern. When the organ, Plotinus said, is detached from its pattern, it is in pain, and its whole effort is to get back to the pattern. In our treatment, we definitely and deliberately attach the idea to the pattern. The practitioner thinks a thought in the field of simultaneous unity. That thought is attached within him to that which identifies it with the action of Cosmic Law.

We start with the idea that man is Spirit. He is perfect. We go beyond the field of psychology in that we identify the patient with the living Spirit within him. There is one Life, that Life is God. Now we detach every thought that contradicts that, on the theory that thoughts are things and that one will neutralize the other and dissolve the idea. You don't treat the effect; you treat the cause, until there arises in your mind a conclusion which is at least more harmonious, happier, and more spiritual and unified than the concept which produced the distress. This is the theory of spiritual healing. It has nothing to do with sending out thoughts. It has nothing to do with holding thoughts. It has nothing to do with influencing anyone; and never in a treatment do you go any further about your patient than to know you are treating a certain person. All of your statements, all of your thoughts, all of

*William Ralph Inge (1860–1954), English prelate, educator, and author.

your words, all of your ideas, all of your feelings are something you do inside yourself—for him.

I believe there are blocks in us which prevent us from doing better work. We have to realize that if there is a Cosmic energy flowing, we didn't create it. If there is a universal Principle acting, we didn't even stimulate it. Self-existence—the two greatest words in our whole philosophy or in any philosophy—is the Principle we are dealing with. It is that which exists by virtue of Its own being, acts by virtue of Its own announcement, and, out of Its movement in action, creates the Law through which the action operates. The Law produces the object of the action automatically through a field of mathematically enforced creativity. As Descartes* said, "I think, therefore I am."

Here is something that nothing can account for. Science, art, religion cannot produce one atom of reality. They can only reveal the atom produced or use the energy caught from the Cosmos itself and individualize it for specific purposes. We define the Cosmos as the Great Circle and the individual as the little circle. The individual is the Circle brought to a point of differentiation in experience, accumulating all of the psychological blocks—so that finally, as Wordsworth† said, he forgets that "celestial palace whence he came."

We are trying to clear the track with the purposive concept that there has to be a self-existent Reality at the center of everything. Everything that is must have a pattern.

---

*René Descartes (1596–1650), French mathematician and philosopher.
†William Wordsworth (1770–1850), English poet.

All patterns are generically universal, and they are individualized in us.

According to the known laws of psychology, which we do not deny, if we attach the libido to a greater purposiveness, if we tie the mind of the individual back to God, it will some day prove to be the perfect science.

3

Wednesday 30 January 1952

"IT'S THE MIND YOU'RE HEALING"
SPIRITUAL THERAPEUTICS

JUNG'S STATEMENT that it doesn't make any difference what the psychologist *says*, it is what he *thinks* that will register with the patient, is an important one in metaphysical mind healing. There is no use in saying any word unless it has meaning, unless it falls spontaneously from our own thinking.

Spiritual mind healing is based on an assumption different from anything else. In no way does it deny physical or psychological healing. In psychosomatic medicine and in psychological analysis, the endeavor is to find the mental equivalent of the physical condition or uncover the "complex" that gives rise to the physical condition. That, in a certain sense, is a part of what we do. But our main endeavor is to reach back and find the spiritual equivalent beyond the mental equivalent or the emotional one. We feel this is drawn from the Universe itself—harmony, peace, joy.

As psychology ties the body back to the mind, so metaphysics ties the mind back to the Spirit. It has to be that way, because we are a product of the Universe. We are all individualized centers of the consciousness of God. The fact that we are demonstrates the Truth. In spiritual mind healing, we tie the mind back to the concept of Spirit, and the one who has the greatest concept of Spirit will be the most efficient spiritual mind healer—because unless the person is established in the consciousness of his oneness with the Spirit, with God, with Life, he has a cure—but not a healing.

There can be a cure without a healing in medicine and in psychology; but the metaphysician, unless he *establishes consciousness*—that means our whole mental action and reaction in the context of a relationship to God, to the Spirit of Truth—also has effected only a cure.

It was Quimby's idea that mind and body are the same thing. That is where modern spiritual mind healing originated. Mind in solution and mind in form are the same thing. But there is a "higher wisdom" which is used to tell the mind about itself and to draw down the spiritual equivalents of the spiritual body. The spiritual equivalent of the circulation of blood is the circulation of divine Life through everything. The spiritual equivalent of the heart is the center of Love, of affection, and of Life.

If there is no troubled mind, there will be no troubled heart. If there is no congestion in the mind, there will be no congestion in the body. The whole process of spiritual mind healing is to present an argument which culminates in a realization based on the concept of perfection and wholeness. The subconscious reaction of all history provides, probably, a subjective or psychic pattern which is its highest estimate of harmony; and, in all probability, what we do is to bring out of a condition that which the consensus of opinion has agreed is normal and harmonious. That would be good enough—if we could do it!

The practitioner in our field practices spiritual mind healing because he knows that the mind in its dual aspect (liquid and solid) is identical—whether you say, "All is Mind and its infinite manifestation,"* or whether you say, as Spinoza† said, "I don't think that mind is one thing and matter another. I think they are the same thing." The Bible says: "Things that are seen are not made of things which do appear, as the invisible things of God from the foundation of the world are the things manifest by the visible."

Quimby said mind is matter in solution, and matter is mind in form. Mind as solution and as form is akin to the conscious and subconscious processes, the creative Thing and the way It creates—mind in its dual aspect. Substance is the matter of Spirit, and through the action of mind, that substance is molded into form, takes form, and is the body. The spiritual practitioner works in this realm. The ancients said, "As above, so below; as below, so above." What's true on one plane is true on all. That's fundamental. The image and the reflection are the same thing.

In our textbook, written about 25 years ago,‡ I took time to explain what the Spirit is, where It is, and what the spiritual element in us is. The only thing we can think of as being the Spirit in us must be that about us which is conscious. It is unfolding, evolving, reaching up and out to that which is gradually coming down into it with

---

*Mary Baker Eddy, in *Science and Health*.
†Benedict de Spinoza (1632–1677), Dutch philosopher.
‡"25 years ago" refers to the first edition of *The Science of Mind* (1926).

greater awareness. In the realm of Spirit, there must be the divine pattern of everything that is; and our mind does have access to these divine patterns.

It isn't that we look at them or image them or visualize them; it is that in every spiritual mind treatment, we not only refute, deny, negate the subjective cause of the physical effect, but we supply the spiritual equivalent for the mind, viewing both cause and effect as equal, identical, and equivalent. It is impossible to divorce the highest form of mental healing from some adequate concept of spiritual realization.

The analyst analyzes by observing a physical effect and going from that to penetrate a psychic, invisible, subconscious cause and bring it to the light of day or self-awareness, where it explains itself away by certain rationalization. The psychologist does *not* find the thing which is independent of this particular chain of cause and effect. Personally, I am convinced that the thing within us which enables us to be aware is as much of the Spirit that is incarnated in us as we now know—and that it reaches into higher levels. It reaches out and up and in deeper and brings more and more awareness to the point of our conscious objectivity. You start from the very external and penetrate to the very internal and find that, in a certain sense, they are the same thing.

The ancients said, "I am that which Thou art, and Thou art that which I am." Jesus said, "It is not I but the Father within me; . . . yet the Father is greater than I." The very fact that a psychologist or a scientist can observe a phenomenon of nature (a cause producing an effect), that he can analyze it, shows that the only thing we know anything about, that knows anything—and knows that it knows, or can reflect on what it knows with awareness—is that consciousness which can accept or reject, which can analyze and decide. That is what we call our conscious faculty. It may seem strange to say that our conscious faculty is the Spirit within us.

When we are dealing with the Law of Mind in action, we are dealing with something where the only self-awareness rests in what we call the Spirit or the Self-Consciousness. I believe *our* self-consciousness, as limited as it is, is still the only evidence we have. That evidence extends itself in all directions, into higher and higher realms; but no matter how high the realms, it carries the knowledge of the lower realms with it, because one is linked with the other in sequence. The higher vitalizes the lower, and the higher form of intelligence governs the lower, even if it's our subconscious mind. But remember: there is no such thing as a subconscious or subjective reaction, in a field of creative Intelligence, that acts like a mind and is a Mind principle.*

What we call "our" subconscious mind is merely a universal medium in which we all live and which reacts to the thought of each one of us according to the way we think; but it is always *one thing*. In our teaching it is very definitely explained that the subconscious part of us reacts to the conscious. Intelligence acts as law that is intelligent, but not conscious.† Form, then, is merely the externali-

---

*I.e., individuality does not entail subjective separateness, or "minds many."

†Dr. Holmes' special sense of *conscious* here is perhaps clarified by (e.g.) "Soul is without *conscious* consciousness, but is conscious in relationship to the impressions it has received" (SOM 96:4; see also 91:3–92:2).

zation of the law that is intelligent but not conscious, so that it knows *how* to do what it is doing, but doesn't know *what* it is doing.

Unless we expect to find such mechanics and such mathematics in the Law of Mind in action, we cannot expect to find such a thing as a Law of Mind in action. That is why we say this is not a faith healing, although the faith used is a potent factor. "It is done unto you *as* you believe." Jesus synthesized, brought together, unified, explained. He understood why it was that people could go to any shrine and if they had belief, there was always something operating on that belief. It would *have* to be done unto them as they believed—a Cosmic force operating on them. As Troward said, "The only way it can do anything for us is by doing it through us." That's what we hold. That's what's back of spiritual mind treatment.

There are two ways of treating. Quimby discovered that, with his "argument,"* he presented the evidence to Mind or to the Mind Principle. The argument reaches a level to change the thought form; but realization brings that level down to substantiate a new basis of thinking. The argument dislodges the thought: that is the cure. Now there must come that influx of spiritual awareness, in order that this dual unity† may be tied back to its own spiritual pattern.

How do we know there is such a spiritual pattern? Spiritual patterns exist, inwardly and logically. We would not be here if they didn't. You can't get something out of nothing: the very fact that we are here shows that they

---

*Basically, "a process of mental reasoning" (SOM 170:4).
†I.e., "choice, volition . . . and automatic reaction" (SOM 42:6).

exist. When you give a spiritual treatment, you are doing something that is out of the ordinary. You are introducing the spiritual equivalent into mental conditions which produce physical effects. It cannot be done on any other basis. People say, "I don't want to do this, I don't want to be religious; it's all in the realm of psychology." It is *not* all in the realm of psychology. Its *effect* is, but its *act* is not. You see, no psychologist has analyzed the Spirit; and most of their analysis has been with abnormal people. Therefore, I should say, there is no reason to suppose that psychology knows any more about spiritual normality than you or I. They have not treated it.

Our treatment must *do* something! You are giving a definite, specific treatment for a definite, specific person. Everything you say, whether the person is sitting before you or is absent, is about that person. It is always *about* him, never *to* him. I have never used the word *you* in a treatment and never expect to. If you will watch carefully, the moment you use the word *you*, you block your treatment. It's impossible to avoid it, because you are wondering if "you" is getting it. You block the freedom of your own thought. Instead, you make your declaration, your affirmation of what ought to be. And you deny what seems to be.

What really happens is that the affirmation and the denial build up a realization or recognition in your mind about this person. Therefore the treatment should end in an affirmation or a realization. As we said the other night, at the core of every neurosis are four things: a sense of *rejection*, the cause of which is a sense of *guilt*, the cause of which is a sense of *insecurity*, the cause of which is a sense of *anxiety*. Now this is very good. We've learned a lot from psychology as to how to proceed in metaphysics. It is entirely scientific, if you're treating somebody for the first time, or yourself for the first time, to remove all sense of guilt. That's why Jesus forgave people their sins. He had a definite purpose in forgiving sin, because it was a block. What you are trying to do in a healing is to get rid of all the blocks so the spiritual equivalent can come down through the mind into the body.

Jung said in *Modern Man in Search of a Soul* that in 35 years of treating people from all over the world he had had few Catholics. They get a clearance through confession—they get forgiveness. They believe in the authority back of their forgiveness, and, when they accept it, it is valid for them. It is scientific: it removes a block in the consciousness of the all-pervasive goodness of Life.

You see, they are tying people back to God, a God they don't have to be afraid of. Perfect love casts out fear. You've got to incorporate in this treatment the idea of divine forgiveness, the idea that there isn't anything in the Universe that holds anything against them. Not every practitioner does this—but every practitioner should be taught to do it. He will be more successful if he does.

You may remember I said the other night that if the analyst has a block in his own consciousness of which he is not aware, when he arrives at the same block in the consciousness of his patient, he will stop. That's why Jesus asked, "Can the blind lead the blind?" "'Physician, heal thyself.'" In psychology and metaphysics, strangely enough, all healing is self-healing, no matter who you are working for. You "forgive" him. He gains assurance that there is nothing to be afraid of: you heal him of fear. His great fear is of God, whether he knows it or not. You tie him back to God.

These are statements that you make in your treatment: There is no fear, no condemnation, no judgment. There is no Hell. There isn't any Purgatory. When I am treating an orthodox person, I ask him about his beliefs. You don't have to be so much concerned about healing the disease: that's an effect of the mind. It's the *mind* you're healing. Maybe a man believes in purgatory and the devils and Satan and all the nonsense that has been shoved down people's imagination, crowded into their emotional throats. If so, he will always be sick, unhappy, insecure, always have a sense of guilt, anxiety—always be prone to it.

There has to come a clearance at the very root of the matter where the person can come to see there is nothing between God and himself. You can argue it with him objectively, you can explain it to him. When he finally gets a complete clearance, he won't be afraid of life, or of others, or of anything else. There will be no conflicts.

But there will always be inhibitions, psychology has taught us, because, as they say, there is an emotional craving for self-expression flowing from the original unconscious through our conscious and becoming imbued with consciousness, then reacting on itself. Freud said we are born with a life urge and we are born with an equal death urge, and when, having contacted human experience, we pile up more liabilities than we have assets—when we come to the place where we expect more pain than pleasure—the death urge comes into play. We see escape from pain in the oblivion of death. The death urge takes over when the life urge no longer provides the anticipation of more pleasure than pain. It's a true principle psychologically. I haven't a doubt of it.

It's well for us to understand all these psychological

things, because we can fit them into the pattern of our metaphysical treatment and neutralize their effects more definitely. The only trouble with Freud's death urge is not that it isn't psychically true; the only trouble with it, philosophically and cosmically, is that, for all he knew, his "death urge" was not a *death* urge, but something else that the ego knew from the upper realms of consciousness that impinge upon it: that it doesn't have to pass into oblivion to get out of pain, that it has something else to look forward to. It knows it is not going to die.

Jung said that in treating he had never known of a single case of permanent healing without a restoration of spiritual faith. That he says in his book *Modern Man in Search of a Soul*—one of the finest books he ever wrote, and very simple. That is quite a statement from a man who is probably the greatest psychologist that ever lived. It ties right back into what I said earlier. We speak of *spiritual* mind healing, not just psychological mind healing. We believe in psychological mind healing; some of it is used every time we give a treatment. In psychology they say that at the core of the neurosis there is a certain complex or cluster of emotional repressions and hurt feelings, sensitiveness, and a sense of rejection which, often, in order to compensate for its inferiority complex, builds up a superiority complex and begins to bluster and blow. This is what is called aggression. If the complex is removed, all of this will disappear.

There is another thing metaphysics adds to psychology. Jesus understood this when he said, "Who is my mother, my father, brother or sister? Everyone is." There is only one race—the human race. We will never be good metaphysicians while we believe in the superiority of any one person over another. I think Plato's definition of God as Truth, Beauty, and Wisdom is one of the finest I've ever heard. Truth: that which is. Beauty: the harmony of everything. Wisdom: the knowledge of all things.

Now remember, as a spiritual mind healer, whether you're treating yourself or somebody else, you're trying to heal the mind. You don't pay much attention to the body. You find certain congestions—but they are congestions in the mind. You heal the mind, the mind heals the body. You do it by a series of statements backed up by a belief. Each treatment is a spontaneous thing. Each treatment *begins* and *ends*, and it isn't a finished thing until you've drawn the highest conclusion you can, until you've used the most logical argument you can, until you have reached the highest degree of realization.

The Principle upon which it works must be as though a universal ear were listening, because the operation of the mind of this ear is subjective: its powers of reasoning are entirely deductive, never argumentative. Like the ground, it accepts the seed that is put into it and begins to create; and so, when the argument reaches the point of self-conviction, of self-assurance, of self-acceptance on the part of the practitioner, it produces this reaction in the Law that knows neither patient nor practitioner beyond the ability of the patient or the practitioner to know himself.

I do not think that the Law of Mind in action knows us beyond our ability to know ourselves—other than as it is tied into the cosmic pattern which knows everything generically, but not individually. We will take that up later. What we want to do now is to get at the methods. So—if we forgive people, that's the starting-point. We

*forg*ive them by assuring ourselves *for* them that everything is all right.

The next thing is belief in immortality. You might
wonder what this has to do with spiritual mind healing,
but I've practiced it for 40 years and it has *everything*
in the world to do with it. You can heal a person of a
headache, a cramp, you can make him feel better, but
why does he come back year after year, if he is healed?
We'll have to admit that both in psychology and in our
metaphysics nine-tenths of our work is *curing* and not
healing. I don't say that critically; I'm just saying that's
the way it is. What we must aim toward is a *healing*.
There is no healing until the consciousness of the patient
is consicously one with the Spirit.

We have to assure him that he is going to live forever,
somewhere. Life is. It cannot die. People must come to
understand that they are immortal, and immortal *now*—
that the Universe holds nothing against them. You can
explain it to them logically and say there is no sin. Sin and
salvation are two ends of one morbidity, one psychological complex.

Because people have what psychology calls an emotional bias, it creates an intellectual blind-spot. You wonder why intelligent people can believe in Hell. Back in the
unconscious is an emotional bias: they were brought up
to believe it. Their whole reaction has been to it. Even
when the Cosmic urge of self-expression flows through
them, it has to interpret itself according to their intellect
and emotional bias and becomes what we call an intellectual blind-spot. It's impossible for such people to think
straight. It's like our political parties. One is just as good
as the other, but nobody believes it. We all have certain
biases. It's what creates intolerance.

We see people who are intolerant, and they are mean and ugly. They have to be forgiven. They have to get over these things. They are not well. I've been treating a very tough case of arthritis—because the guy was mean. He didn't *know* he was mean. There are certain emotional reasons why he *was* mean. I didn't treat his arthritis at all. I treated to know that there is a flexibility, a generosity, a spirit of love and tolerance and understanding, and that there is nothing that can settle where it does not belong. Everything is liquid, everything is fluid. Why shouldn't the power that put this thing there take it away?

We have to heal people of the fear of death and the fear of life and the fear of God and the fear of the devil. How are we going to do it? By *ourselves* coming to know that life is immortal. Something in us knows it to be true.

We must come to know that God is Love; we'll *have* to know it. I know it. I can't prove it, but I know it.

We must also come to have faith and conviction that spiritual power exists, that a spiritual and mental law operates upon our convictions—and that in the Law is the self-determination of the fact or the mechanics of its own evolution. We don't make anything happen. We don't hold thoughts. We explain all this *to ourselves* for the benefit of the person we are treating—and he gets it. I think the thing that happens is (just as water will reach its own level and overflow): *what we think for this person simultaneously reaches the level of his consciousness.* It has to work through his consciousness, but it doesn't work through his consciousness by our working on *his* consciousness.

You see, we start with the assumption that in this universal Mind everyone comes to a point of self-awareness as an individual, and each one individualizes God in a unique way. By the way, no metaphysician could ever be a Communist. He would hate it worse than anyone, because it is directly contrary to the two great laws: the unity in which everything is rooted, and the diversity through which everything is expressed. That is the spirit of democracy.

There are two things that make democracy: (1) *The fact that no two things are alike* (making it necessary that the Cosmic Mind present Itself to each in a little different way—the unity that never means uniformity). (2) *The uniqueness of the presentation* through the incarnation of the Infinite at the points of manifestation of limitless individualizations, each one of which is not an *individual,* but an *individualization.*

Our whole theory is that every person individualizes God. Every person in Spirit is perfect. Jesus understood that. He said, "Be ye therefore perfect even as your Father in heaven." It was to your "Father" in your "heaven," or the Higher Self, to which Jesus prayed—that which is the Cosmic Self now manifesting as the individual self. The two selves are one. God is over all, in all, through all, and all in all. I am that I am. I am that which Thou art. Thou art that which I am. They all say it in various ways. So our basis is perfect God, perfect Man, perfect Being. There is the basis for your argument, the basis for your treatment, the basis for your realization.

All the things that happen from the time you start with that premise are a neutralizing of that which blocks the Cosmic flow. Do you see how that would be? That's what happens in metaphysics; it's really what happens in psychology. Mrs. Eddy* said, "Destroy the enemy and leave

*Mary Baker Eddy (1821–1910), founder of Christian Science.

the field to God." Jesus said, "Be ye perfect even as your Father." And remember his prayer: "Our Father, which art in heaven, hallowed be thy name; thy kingdom come, thy will be done on earth, as it is in heaven." That's the law of parallels.

Jesus was saying that when the kingdom of God comes on earth and the will of God is done on earth, then that which is in heaven, which is already there, will find its correspondence on earth. That the time will come when we are aware that it is now here, and to *us* not until that time, because the divine offering is forever made. Our whole process of evolution is the accumulation of our acceptances of that which is forever given, and forever forgiven by the same token of givingness as we forgive. This is the way it is. We heal people of the fear of Hell and damnation, of God, man, and the devil. There is nothing to be afraid of. Perfect love casts out all fear, including fear of the thought of death or dying. We must heal people of everything that denies the supremacy of God.

Because you and I have not yet arrived at a complete supremacy of good, we have to do the best we can. We do have to hitch our earthly wagon to a spiritual star, because if we don't we're going to hitch it to a make-believe life, something that has no light at all. The only light there is is the Light Eternal. We have to tie our minds to spiritual verity—there is no other way. That is why we speak of spiritual mind healing. The psychologists have told us much that helps. If a person is always full of biases, we have to treat him for power, we have to know that way back in there, there wasn't anything that ever happened to him that set him against people. He gets a superiority complex because he had an inferiority complex. In reality, even in psychology, there isn't such a thing as a superiority complex—it is an inferiority complex making a noise so it won't scare itself to death. The aggression is merely the almost unconscious act of protection. At the core of every neurosis are rejection, guilt, insecurity, anxiety. We should definitely cover all these points in most of our healing.

If thousands of people have spent years in work and endeavor to find out what's wrong with the mental man, just as doctors have with the physical man, it's only common sense for us to take advantage of everything they've learned—and we find that most metaphysicians almost automatically have been cooperative with it. Out of their experience we have known that it is almost impossible for a person to get a complete psychic* clearance.

Have any of you ever read the *Sutras of Patanjali*? Patanjali was the man who set about, 3500 years ago, collecting the ancient teachings of India. He said everything I'm talking about. In our field it has always been said that if you saw the error and knew what you wanted to change, it was that much easier. We have to do it by talking through the intellect back into the emotions. It is generally conceded to be effective only when, through a subtlety of mental direction, the practitioner lets the patient unfold it: he has got to come to self-awareness. *But we don't do it that way.* We sideswipe it, neutralize it, short-circuit it. It is like an electric energy that can be short-circuited. Rawson† wrote a book—*Life Understood*, a great metaphysical work—in which he spoke of

---

*I.e., of the psyche.
†Frederick Rawson (1859–1923), English metaphysician and author.

short-circuiting, maybe because he had been an electrical engineer.

There is as yet no philosophy back of psychology. It isn't connected up with anything Cosmic; and yet everything in the Universe is. Psychology has no individual harmony or individual mathematics. We work on the assumption that there is only one subconscious field operating through all the people in the world and that each individual subconscious mind is not a separate and distinct mind (and certainly not an entity) but is merely subconscious *reaction*, in a field of Mind, to everything this person has thought, said, and done, and probably to the whole race consciousness localized in him, but in itself spreading everywhere. Therefore, you can neutralize it wherever you are. That's the difference between the two approaches and the difference between their methods.

Because this is the principle of our method, your absent treatment and your present treatment are the same thing, and all treatment is the same in that it merely identifies itself with the person you want to treat.

Now a few moments for a question, because we're in the center of the subject. I want this clear, because we're not going to have time to talk more about it.

Q. When a treatment is given for a person who is absent, do they have to be receptive to it?

A. I'm glad you asked that. Receptivity has nothing to do with it. All you are doing is declaring the spiritual truth about some individual. It cannot influence him. It cannot hurt him. It can do nothing but liberate him. It probably removes that much more ignorance; and ignorance is all that's wrong with anything. The ancients call the whole problem of evil *the great ignorance*. Jesus healed many people who did not know he was treating them—the centurion's servant, for example. He knew he was not manipulating anyone. He was knowing the truth.

The truth about hate is love. We can find the spiritual equivalent of any negation by turning to its exact opposite. The truth about fear is faith, the truth about hell is heaven, the truth about the devil is God, the truth about loneliness is inclusion, the truth about lack is abundance, the truth about bad circulation is that Life circulates, the truth about heart trouble is that there is only one Heart, and It is never troubled. You see, Truth has got to be that which is universal, Cosmic, and automatically flowing through everything that is individual or personal.

That brings up another question. You don't have to know where the person is or what he is doing. You don't care. Your word is given in your own mind. Your treatment begins and ends in your own mind. The idea that a person you are treating must have faith is all right if he is depending on faith healing, certainly. But this is *not* faith healing. The more faith *we* have in it, the better it will work, probably; but in a certain sense, if we could come to the place where we no longer had to have faith in it, because we knew it was true, then we would use it with complete assurance. Do we or do we not have faith when we press a button to get electric light? We do. Yes, but it's more than faith. We have *conviction*—out of experience, out of usage. We know that it will work that way. And so we know that there will appear in the experience of the patient something at the level of our own recognition.

Now I will say this, although it's a theory: some people seem easier to work with than others. With others, you don't seem to get anywhere. There may be a kind of rejection that isn't reached; I don't know. But the principle will have to be the same—because if there appears to be a rejection, you must begin to work to know that there is none. If there appears to be a lack of confidence, you begin to work for it, because in spiritual mind treatment every objective thing and every psychological thing that denies the spiritual pattern you theoretically turn into a thought, and then you erase the thought and use its opposite.

Now, is there anyone here who thinks he could not give a good treatment? Is there anyone who would doubt his ability to give as good a treatment as anyone who ever lived could give? You see, all healing is impersonal. It has nothing to do with you or with me. It isn't our will, it isn't our wish, it isn't even our desire. We *will* to do it, we *want* to do it, we *desire* to do it; but the healing itself is a clearing up of something in one's own consciousness for someone else, always based on the thought of perfect God, perfect Man, perfect Being—no matter what appears. We work toward that end or objective as best we may. I don't think we should be disappointed if we don't heal everyone. But we should never deviate or depart from the One Thing.

And there is one other thing I want to say in closing. There is something about this that makes only people who believe in spiritual things good practitioners. Only people who have a great love for people make good practitioners. Only people whose tolerance has passed into understanding make good practitioners. Only people who have a natural or developed inclination and a conscious and subjective ability to feel the invisible make good practitioners.

I'm not talking about anything queer or occult. All I'm saying is this: will you ever have a great artist unless he has a great appreciation of beauty? It's impossible. You'll never have a great musician without a great appreciation of that which makes music.

It's an interesting thing to me that all our music, our art, and our religion come from the same source. All art came out of religion. All religion came out of intuition. All intuition is the self-perception of the infinite norm knowing in us. You cannot separate spiritual concepts, which in our emotions and our intellects become our religions—and they're all right.

You cannot divorce that concept from spiritual mind healing and get very far. It is only the one who is able to abandon himself with a complete surrender to the genius of that spark of consciousness which seemed to come with us, that we had nothing to do with, who makes the best healer. But everyone has this spark, everyone has this love, everyone has this understanding beyond tolerance, everyone has this rhythm, this harmony—everyone has it just because he is here. Therefore it exists alike, somewhere at the depths of our being, in all people—to be reached by feeling, by objective conversation, by sympathy and tolerance and kindness and human understanding, by love and attention and all the little things of life.

4

<u>Wednesday 6 February 1952</u>

"THE UNIVERSE
DOESN'T TOIL"
TREATING TO IMPROVE CONDITIONS

T HE IMPORTANCE of our lesson tonight—which we
might call the technique of treating ourselves and
others for betterment of conditions (social relationships,
personal life, personality problems)—is, first of all, fundamentally to ourselves as individuals. It is also the im-
pact that we have upon our environment.

The whole thought and idea of war* would disappear
from the human consciousness if there were enough people who understood the Principle we're talking about—
and used it. The world would solve its problems because
enough divine guidance would come down into the intellect and the emotions. The solution lies in spiritual
awareness. Spiritual awareness to us is the conscious in-
terior awareness that we are one with the divine Presence—the source of inspiration, illumination, intelligent
guidance, and the consciousness that there *is* such a divine

---

*The United States was then at war with North Korea.

Presence, that there *must* be a universal Spirit and Mind which we use—and an awareness that there is a Law of Mind in action which acts mathematically, mechanically, but intelligently, having no purpose or intention of its own, but apparently following the consciousness which (mostly unconsciously) directs it. The awareness that each one of us, individually, has access to Intelligence as Spirit, and to the reactive, creative Intelligence as Law, is the whole basis of our teaching.

The Bible says: "If ye know these things, happy are ye if ye do them." One trouble with the metaphysical movement is that, while we don't know very much, we *do* know way beyond what we are using. The reason for that is simple. The most difficult thing in the world is to get a person to believe a treatment *is* a treatment. The most difficult thing is to keep people from becoming confused and arriving at a place where they never know what they believe—and never use it. The strongest consciousness in a group of people that can exist will be found in a group of people who unitedly agree on certain fundamental principles and techniques for practice in this field, and then individually, collectively, and specifically use them and never stop using them. One of our greatest troubles is a tendency to think it must be something different from what it is.

We're talking about principles that exist, principles as they operate, techniques as they must be used. We know how they work. Our Law is a Law of Mind in action, creative thinking, and it is impossible for anyone to get the best out of it without using it consistently and persistently and very simply, accepting, as every scientific mind must accept, that principles do not change or alter their course to suit our convenience. *We* are subject to *them*. *They* are not subject to *us*. Even though we use a higher power and a superior Intelligence, it is not higher in that it is different. It is higher only in that it is greater than we are. And the superior Intelligence is not superior in essence, but only in its universality, which we cannot grasp all at one time.

We must come to accept this as a new field. Out of the last 50 years of research, our relationship to the universal Principle of Mind and to the laws of Mind has been as definitely outlined as any other science. The leaders have proceeded on the basis that the techniques now known, understood, and used, while they may not be perfect and while much may be added to them, are today the best we know.

Someone said to me the other day, "I never give but one treatment. I believe it's wrong to keep giving more than one treatment." I said, "When you're only going to give one treatment, be absolutely certain, before you finish, that your patient is well or that the condition is met— because if that doesn't happen, either you haven't given the treatment, or the treatment was wrong." This is not a method whereby we say that people are not sick, or poor, or weak, or unhappy. This is not something where we say "Peace, Peace" when there is no peace. Our motto is: to know and to do. Our theory is simplicity itself, and I want to deal with that theory tonight from the standpoint of the control of conditions.

One night many years ago when I was trying to figure this thing out and reading everything in the world—occultism, spiritualism, theosophy, Christian Science, New Thought, everything—someone asked me to treat him. I remember I sat up for about two hours. It was midnight and the first time I ever really knew what a treatment was. You can only discover it for yourself by making it work, because what happened then seemed like a miracle to me.

The man woke up in the middle of the night and he felt his whole spine readjust itself—the whole mechanical thing. There was no question but that it was the result of the treatment. I was treating just to know that everything was in place there. That was the first time that the dynamic power of this thing appealed to my imagination. The important thing is that we recognize the Power, that we realize our relationship to it, that we accept it in simplicity.

We must recognize that our point of contact with divine Mind as divine Presence, and divine Mind as Principle, is always at the center of our own being, through our own being, and proceeding from it. Our being is merely a point where the infinite Being, like a wave of the ocean, comes into self-expression and self-experience, no doubt backed by a Cosmic urge or necessity. Because I believe that the libido of psychology is merely that stream of the universal urge to self-expression, I call it the divine urge.

In all the courses in metaphysics that were ever written, there are not more than a half-dozen things of vital importance, although they all break down into many other things to give us the reasons for what we do. First of all, there is the Father Spirit, the masculine; second, the Mother Spirit, the feminine or the Soul, the Law of Mind in action. "They that worship the Father must worship him in Spirit and in truth," said Jesus. We are one with the creative Law of Self-Existence, we are one with the Body of God, and we should be able to reach back through our thinking to that which is original, all-powerful, omnipotent—God—and cause the action of divine Spirit to move on our own mind constantly and subjectively. We are manifestations of invisible causes. The smart thing to do is to accept what all the great and good and wise have taught. They all teach the same thing, they all practice the same way, and one gets just as good results as another.

In considering the control of conditions, your whole treatment is based on two things: *identification* and *reciprocal action of the Spirit or the Law*. First of all, though, there has to be the belief and the recognition, because you can't speak a word with sincerity unless you believe it. So first of all we have the recognition. Jesus based everything on belief—belief in a higher Power. We use a higher Power every time we use a law of Nature, whatever it may be.

The next is identification with the higher Power. I am a part of it; it is a part of me. There is one Mind, that Mind is God, that Mind is my mind now. There is one Life, that Life is God, that Life is my life now. You see, your whole action takes place in the mind, the movement of the mind upon itself. That's the action and reaction of the whole Universe, the movement of Intelligence on itself and of itself, projecting and creating that which it conceives through the Law of its own self-existent recognition, its self-animating, self-propelling, self-sustaining, self-energizing realization.

The first axiom of reason is: "The truth is that which is."* We have to accept, just as we accept gravity, that there are self-existent spiritual and mental truths which, when known, will automatically make us free. "Ye shall know the truth, and the truth shall make you free." So there is, first, conviction, belief, faith, acceptance. Next, identification with that which is certainly greater than our intellect, greater than the sum total of human intelligence. The Bible says: "Who made the ear, shall He not hear? Who made the eye, shall He not see? Who made the understanding, shall He not understand?"

Jesus stood in front of the tomb of Lazarus and said, "Father, I thank Thee that Thou hearest me." That's recognition. "And I know that Thou always hearest me"— that's identification and unification. Then He turned and told Lazarus to come out. That's command.† He knew he was using a law. He had such conviction of that Law that he said, "Heaven and earth shall pass away, but the Law shall not pass away."

Everything that Jesus taught, every parable, every message, everything he uttered, all of his sermons—such as the Sermon on the Mount—were adaptations of different ways to show us the relationship that we have to the universal Mind, Spirit, Intelligence, and Law. There are

*"Truth is what is and not what we think. . . . It is not by merit of any virtue we possess that truth is truth; we are only fortunate if we see it and understand it and accept it!"—*Holmes Papers*, vol. 2, pp. 187, 189.

†Dr. Holmes sometimes gave *command* as the third essential element in treatment; more commonly he cited *realization*, or *acceptance*. The context usually governed his choice. By *command* he implied *authority*. See *Think Your Troubles Away* (Misc. Writings of Ernest Holmes, vol. 3), p. 69.

no exceptions. His parables are drawn from Nature. "As you sow, so shall you reap." In the story of the Prodigal Son, the Father comes out to meet the Son; because the moment the Son turns to his Father, the Father turns to the Son. The turning of the Son to his Father is recognition at the level of the Son's ability to know the Father. "It is done unto you *as* you believe," said Jesus. It is the same thing as Emerson's law of parallels, or what Swedenborg* meant by the law of correspondences; what the Hermetic teaching meant by "As above, so beneath." What's true on one plane is true on all.

The Prodigal Son dreamed up a separation from the Infinite—and as he awoke and came to himself, he turned to the Father, and the Father to him. We call this the law of reciprocal action. The seed you plant acts by reciprocal action, responds by a co-response, takes the thing from the darkness of its creative medium and shoves it up into the light. "These signs," said Jesus, "shall follow them that believe."

If you've read Troward, this is what he means by universal subjectivity—the feminine principle in nature. It's the Isis of the Egyptian mythology. It is what is called the Mother Principle, or the "Father-Mother God." This was called the Womb of Nature in the first few centuries of the Catholic church; they recognized it as the Soul of the Universe, the Womb of Nature giving birth to creation —the subjective Intelligence which knows *how* to do without knowing *that* it's doing it. The soil doesn't know that it's making an oak tree. It responds to the acorn by corresponding to the pattern which is in the acorn. The

*Emanuel Swedenborg (1688–1772), Swedish philosopher and religious writer.

Bible talks of "when the plant was in the seed before the seed was in the ground."

So this is the treatment. Nothing can come out of the treatment that doesn't go into it. For instance, you can plant a melon seed and you won't get cucumbers. You'll get *melon*, and you'll get a multiplicity of response of the same type—it won't convert itself into another type. Everything in Nature is definite, coherent, exact, mathematical, and mechanical in its formation. This is the subjective state of our thought; it's the sum total of our thinking. It is a mind principle operating through us. This is the treatment; this is the medium; and this is the demonstration. This is the belief; this is what it does to you; and this is what it yields.

But there is our objective word, our choice. It is not everyone who says "Lord, Lord" who enters into the kingdom of wholeness, but rather the one who has harmonized himself with the nature of that kingdom. In other words, your treatment is *upon yourself*, no matter what you're working for. Theoretically, we ought so to live and think that our objective thinking is not interfered with. Every man should speak consciously from an intuitional center in the Mind of the Infinite. That's the ultimate. That's what we strive toward. We should theoretically always know the Truth. If we did, we'd make no mistakes.

It's strange to speak of an infinite Intelligence as though it hadn't any sense; but the creative soil doesn't know the seed you put into it. Electric energy doesn't know it's made into light. We've got to think of an infinite Medium —Mind, Intelligence, Creativity—that knows how to create conditions and yet doesn't know that it knows how to create conditions. We've got to think, then; and how *shall* we think so that it never makes anything for us that isn't good? We wouldn't want such a creative Medium at our disposal to be used in such a way as to destroy us. We are saying, everywhere you look in Nature such principles exist. The destructive use of any principle destroys the one who uses it. That's the old theory of good and evil.

Jesus didn't say the world was bad. He just said, "I've overcome it. It is subject to me now. I'm no longer subject to it." He added that the reason he did as he did was to please the Father. In the parable of the Prodigal Son, Jesus was telling us the way it works in our relationships, in our relationship to God and the Law. He said the same thing to the man who died with him on the cross: "In a few minutes thou shalt be with me in Paradise." This is the reciprocal action. This is the law of Life. If today our thoughts cancel out the mistakes of yesterday by uprooting them and no longer indulging in them—*they are not there!* Jesus did not teach an *easy* salvation; he taught a *sure* one. He did not teach a *soft* principle; he taught an *immutable* one, *impartial*, one that always works.

One of our great troubles is that it's difficult to get people to realize that through a process of faith and realization they can instantly know the Truth. There is a technique which is cumulative and which will finally produce on the subjective side of our lives enough affirmative action to cause the reaction. A treatment is not just wishing somebody well. You must do something to change the condition. We've got to realize that whatever this Thing is, it's God, Love, Reason, Truth, Beauty, Wisdom, Power, Balance, Poise, Sanity. It has never made mistakes. As the old Jewish Talmud says: "What evil there is that betideth thee is of thyself. The good that betideth thee is of God." We've got to realize that; and that's all we teach.

It's difficult to get people to realize that a treatment has a beginning, a middle, and an end. If by one grand sweep of our consciousness we can revolutionize a man's whole life, or our own, and change a whole situation just by saying, "It's done," then that's the criterion: nobody's going to argue with the fellow who can do that! If I go down the street and see someone raising the dead, I'm not even going to ask how he does it. I'm going to say, "Brother, just let me sit close to you and see. I know already what it is that does it, but let me see if I can feel how you feel, so I can feel the same way about the Thing that does it—because I know that you have an instantaneous sense of the divine Presence and the operation of the Law of Good, until the one is lost in the other and your whole life is a proclamation of an infinite Self against which there is no judgment."

We all know that, and once in a while our own consciousness rises to a supreme height. Without our ever being aware of it, miracles seem to take place. But more often in your experience and in mine, we find that a series of statements creates a subjective reaction to those statements, which in turn becomes an affirmation in the Law. That's the way treatments are cumulative: mental work counts, and we must work until we get results.

The most difficult thing for people to recognize is that a treatment *is* a treatment. A man says, "I have no friends," and the words are cumulative. People avoid him and never know why they do. Some people are too eager; they don't sit still in that Thing inside of them that is a friend and let the irresistible Law of Good draw by a gravitational force of its own. There are two things that can happen as you treat the man who is friendless: your treatment will automatically attract friends to him while you treat him; but unless during this process his own consciousness is changed, when you stop treating him the action of your thought will stop, because he is unconsciously rejecting it.

While you are treating him to attract friends, treat him to know that he is one with all people: *then there will be a healing*. The other is a *cure*. A cure is good, but a healing is permanent. In doing this, you just put in your own words what you want to happen: he is one with God, he is one with man, he is one with all people, he is one with Life, he is one with all friendship, he is a friend to everyone he meets, and everyone he meets is a friend to him. *He knows this, he is aware of it.* There is no sensitiveness, no timidity, no fear.

You've got to put this into words until the time comes when your radiation needs no words. It is a living, operating at-one-ment or unity. Now the time will come for this person, if he is healed, when he will find he can go from one city to another and make the same kind of friendship he left behind him.

I've watched this thing work in the training of our own practitioners. We've trained over 2,000 here throughout the years, and I've been able to follow 200 or 300 of them. Some have been successful, some haven't. That's like anything else and has nothing to do with the Principle. But

I've been interested in noting the attraction of patients: they attract the patients who come out of the subjective levels of their own* unconscious. Some who are fond of the theatre attract almost wholly theatrical people. People who have been in business and become practitioners are likely to attract business people. That's the way the Law works—it couldn't be otherwise. So after the person who is treated for attracting friends is rightly trained, he will find friends everywhere he goes, because there will be nothing in him to contradict friendship.

Suppose a man comes to you and says, "I don't have any opportunity." *Everywhere he goes there is opportunity!* Put it in words, words that mean something to you. In my radio treatment† I say, "There's an infinite Intelligence that governs and guides and guards. . . ." It's impossible for you and me to recognize a Cosmic truth about ourselves that we refuse to recognize for other people. This is the way the great and the good have taught; because it is only as we identify ourselves with a higher consciousness that a higher potential flows through our minds and reacts on our environment. The time will come for this person you're working for when he will see opportunity everywhere. Then he will be in rhythm with Life.

You pass from physical laws to spiritual laws, and you find them in everything. This is a great law of metaphysics—the law of mental equivalents, of subjective

---

*I.e., the practitioners'.
†Dr. Holmes had a radio program, *This Thing Called Life*, aired on Sundays at 4 P.M.

embodiment, automatically acting at every level of our experience. It is the same law by which water reaches its own level by its own weight. The greatest word in our whole vocabulary is a compound expression of Self-Existence, of Law and Life, and of manifestation.*

Let us suppose that in our experience we are confronted by so many difficulties that each one is a mountain. We're functioning low in the mind: *this* obstructs us and *that* obstructs us. We look at all the obstructions and become so confused that we're pretty nearly crazy. Now we want consciousness to function at its own level by its own weight and automatically rub all of these obstructions out. In denying each one of them, suppose we get up to the place where we look over all of them. There is a state of awareness possible in the mind which rises above all confusion, apprehension, fear, or doubt, and, looking over the obstructions, can dissipate them by the divinity of its own God-like glance.

There is something that can look at an obstruction and look away, just as you can hold a piece of ice in your hand and let it melt away. But we generally get caught about here, don't we? Once in a while we break through. Our endeavor is always to rise and, in the ascent, cancel out each one of these things that present themselves. The method will carry us to where it is transcended by awareness, and automatically the problems will change. There is in us a subjective imagery and an awareness that is equal to what we experience. Emmet Fox wrote of it, and

---

Word and *vocabulary* are not meant literally here but instead refer to *concept in expression* and *frame of reference* respectively.

so did Troward. Troward said, "If you want to be sure you're treating in the Absolute there is a conscious something you feel inside."

First of all, you know that there is nothing—past, present, or future—that limits you or what you're doing. There's nothing existing that you know of now, or that you can imagine in the future, or can remember in the past, that can limit you. Then rise to the pure consciousness of self-existent identification, and that realization you make is now no longer you—it is God in you! And against such there is no law. Paul said that the Law is a schoolmaster bringing us to Christ.

Now let's put this whole thing together, because there are certain abstractions we have to touch upon. We've been talking about treating people for conditions in which they lack friends, or money, or opportunity. It doesn't matter what they lack. You have to have variation or you have monotony, and monotony is insanity. The mountain does not compete with the valley; the valley may be as beautiful as the mountain. You have to have contour or you have sameness, and there *is* no sameness in life. The cactus does not compete with the Joshua tree, nor the rosebush with the sequoia. The contrast is not a contrast of differences in Principle, but the contrast of variations. We have a right to treat for anything that makes a person happy, if it doesn't harm some other person.

Let us be that which we are and "draw the Thing as we see It for the God of Things as They are." If you want to make mudpies, make them. If you like to build skyscrapers, there's nothing wrong with skyscrapers.

*I am tired of planning and toiling in the crowded lives
    of men;
Heart weary of building and spoiling, and spoiling and
    building again.
And I long for the dear old river, where I dreamed my
    youth away;
For a dreamer lives forever, and a toiler dies in a day.**

The Universe doesn't toil.
It flows.

*John Boyle O'Reilly (1844–1890), "The Cry of a Dreamer."

5

"SIMULTANEOUS UNITY AND INSTANTANEOUS DEDUCTION"
THE PSYCHIC REALM

T HE TOPIC tonight is a weird one, something on the "ghost" side of life. Anyone who is not acquainted with the very little that is known about psychic things doesn't know the attempt that is being made to put together the spiritual and mental phenomena that have existed throughout the ages. It would be impossible to give the talk on spiritual illumination next week without this talk tonight, because spiritual illumination is beyond the psychic realm, a principle higher than our subjectivity. We cannot discount the psychic life because it is as much a part of us as is the physical. As a matter of fact, it is more—because mind is soul.

Tonight, I want to discuss what we know and what we do not know; what we're not sure of; and what seems to be in the realm of what is believed—all based on facts that can be verified scientifically and experienced individually as well as more or less collectively, and all of which comes under the general heading of psychic or subjective phenomena.

We think of the realm of the Spirit as that which, in us, is consciously aware of itself, but which conscious awareness seems to expand infinitely. There seems to be no limit to its expansion. I'm not thinking of the Spirit in man as something separated from his conscious faculties, because if it were, we wouldn't have any conscious faculties with which to go in search after this assumption,* and it is only the impingement of this assumption on that in us which is conscious that extends the awareness to that which is Cosmic.

That is our subject for next week.

Right now I want to talk about what seems, perhaps, to be a barrier between our intellect, our objective mind, and our bodies on the one hand, and this universal Spirit on the other—the apparent gulf that seems to be between the two but that in reality is a state of consciousness imposed on us by the Universe itself.

Throughout the ages, people have experienced what today we call psychic phenomena, or what Dr. Rhine calls extrasensory perceptions. He didn't want to use the term psychic phenomena, because to many people that means séances and spiritualism and ghosts and weird voices. He has, under laboratory conditions, demonstrated not something new, but something that all people in the field were familiar with. He demonstrated it in a way that the scientific world cannot repudiate and must finally accept.

This evening I want to examine this whole field and see what we think might be the reason these things happen. For instance, I have on one occasion seen 19 com-

---

*I.e., of the unlimited expansion of conscious awareness.

plete materializations, with weight, substance, dimension, breadth, clothes, shoes, and vocal organs, and enough intelligence to talk under the test conditions of two veteran investigators—Dr. Hill and the late Hamlin Garland.* We are all probably aware of the things that go on in the average séance where people apparently come and talk through a medium. I have worked with Eileen Garrett and Arthur Ford, probably the two greatest mediums living today, and with Dr. Williams and 15 or 20 others. Always some phenomena are produced. The spiritualist, naturally, is convinced that the phenomena are that of discarnate spirits and that everything is exactly as it is said to be.

I'm not saying that it is or is not. That's for you to judge. But I think we have to look for a deeper explanation. The spiritualists believe their friends still are living and accept it, and they're not afraid of what they believe. To believe in a person's sincerity, his integrity, simplicity, and honesty, and to admire his spiritual convictions is one thing; to accept all of his conclusions about the phenomena is quite another thing. I look upon this just as I do the life of prayer. Throughout the ages, people have prayed and have had their prayers answered; but throughout the ages most prayers have *not* been answered, certainly not the way they have been asked.

Then someone comes along and says there is a principle behind prayer. The principle is that when the affirmation is completely accepted by the one who prays, a law is set in motion, or some law operates and tends to cre-

*(1860–1940), American writer and Pulitzer prize winner. His *The Mystery of the Buried Crosses* (1939) dealt with psychic research.

ate the condition which is accepted at the time of the prayer. When you begin to train people to do that consciously, they begin to get results way beyond the realm of chance.

Then you know you have switched over from the field of supposition and superstition and theory of whether something may or may not be true, and you build enough evidence on this side to establish the concept of a scientific principle you can teach to anyone. You have established a neutral, impersonal, plastic, ever-present, responsive, creative, scientific principle which we call *universal Mind responding to us at the level of our embodiment, acceptance, and mental equivalent of it.* This is scientifically established.

We cannot arrive at truth by the denial of fact, but by the *synthesis* of fact, which automatically creates a unification of principles that give rise to a variation of performances* which exist in reality but cannot be interpreted just by their appearance. Dr. von Koerber, one of the most spiritually enlightened persons who ever come to talk to us here, head of the Department of Oriental Civilization at the University of Southern California, told us one day that he had been in a lamasery in Tibet for four years and had become initiated in their mysteries. He has seen levitation. He was amazed when I told him that I had seen it in séances. What we have to do is to try to find out what might be the explanation of all forms of psychic phenomena—whether it be the manifestation of a body temporarily held in form, a spirit rapping a com-

---

*"Variation of performances": i.e., departure from patterns; "in reality": as facts of experience.

munication from a discarnate entity, or whatever. (I believe people do communicate with spirits. I know I have. I just don't believe they are all around us like a swarm of bees all the time.)

We are spirits now, just as much as we ever shall be. Therefore, there is no reason and logic to suppose that as spirits ten years from now we shall be able to do something we cannot do now. It seems very possible to me that we, as spirits now, do unconsciously produce most of these phenomena. These facts we cannot deny, nor can anyone who investigates. The question is not whether the facts are real; it is merely the interpretation of them.

I want to show you what some of these interpretations are. Let's take the idea of remembering. Under certain conditions, anyone can remember anything that ever happened to anyone who ever lived. The field of memory is a universal medium which is timeless, unobstructed, present everywhere. Nothing ever really blocks it. Therefore, if you will just think of it as the universal subjectivity and think of this as your individual being, you will discover that the subconscious mind is not a separated or isolated mind. It is merely the place where you use a subjective law of mind and where, using it, you surround yourself with the reaction. It becomes a point of attraction or repulsion in your polarity in a universal field. We're all psychic, from the standpoint of Principle. One person is not more psychic than another; but for some reason it comes to the surface in some more than in others.

Many of the best exhibitions—the ones I've tried with Arthur Ford and Eileen Garrett—are worked by going into a trance, in order to get rid of every objective thing so that the subjective may come immediately to the surface. In this, everybody you ever knew in your life can come to you, theoretically—one after another. They'll tell you all about themselves, they'll bring to memory things that happened, they'll tell you incidents. I've never known of many cases where the spirits refused to attend. Now that is of very great significance, philosophically and logically; because there's no use our disputing that the phenomena exist.

The question is merely this: *What does it*? I'm not denying that the spirits might be there; I'm not saying they couldn't be there. I'm just saying this: why should they be following me around? Why should they be in continual conscious contact with me? We know that we can psychically contact anyone in the flesh and even know what they are thinking, if there is any reason to do so. I know *I* can; but I never try to do it. As far as I'm concerned, I've always tried to shut the psychic door, because it can become a liability.

The problem, then, is not a problem of the validity of the phenomena; it is merely what explanation we shall accept as being the cause of it. In all probability, the most rational and reasonable cause that is now known is that whenever we think of anyone we've ever known, we can connect up with the memory image of his vibration.

Another group of scientific investigators in Europe several years ago evolved the theory that we must keep away from spiritualism and remain pretty materialistic about it all . . . that when we pass on, we leave a detached personification of that which we were. So far as we know, that personification exists for an indefinite period of time, because these appearances, apparitions, have been seen at certain definite spots for hundreds of years. It appears that whenever the purpose for which they were created or given enough life to execute that mission is achieved, they disappear.

That's what the kahunas of the Hawaiian Islands believed. They called it the middle and the lower self. What they called the higher self had left the body and might exist for generations, but finally would dissolve. The occultists believe that there is a detached astral or etheric body, which is not of the spiritual body, and that it would continue to operate continuously on the physical plane because that is all it ever knew, and that it might obsess or influence people and become the agency for what has been called the obsession of discarnate spirits. Those are among the theories.

Some modern scientists have deduced the same principle that the kahunas had. All of this doesn't come out of nothing. Something happens to our memory, apparently, and we still exist after we have gone on, in a field which is one with this memory. If we are clairvoyant, if we are psychic, we get an impression and apparently it can be carried to the extent of audible words, or clauraudience. This is not a psychic hallucination: you can take it down on a record and play it over and over again. I have some records of someone who would come and sing, and records of a Catholic priest who would say the Mass in Latin. The priest was a friend of mine, but the singer we never could identify. It was *not* an illusion.

The spiritualists say, "What could be more simple, more direct, and more rational than to accept it all?" If someone comes to you and says, "I am your grandmother and I'm interested in you," why not accept it as a fact? A medium said to me about two weeks after my mother

died, "We were at a séance the other night and your
mother came back." I said, "That's interesting. What did
she say?" She said that my mother was very confused. I
said, "You've got the wrong woman. She wasn't confused
the few moments before she passed away, and I don't
think she was a few moments after she got wherever she
was going."

I knew a medium who used to diagnose people. If you
could get a correct psychic diagnosis, it would probably
be more correct than any physical one, because you're
dealing with a mind principle that knows what is going
on in its own field. This medium would see thought-forms
and she would, in her own imagination and with physical acts, appear to wrest them from the patients. She'd see
them as a cat, a dog, a wolf. That might have been a symbol that the mind presented to the mind, and she at least
did some very remarkable things in exorcising them and
getting rid of them.

We don't go very far into this in our field, but we do
not want to overlook the fact that all of these things happen and that they have happened throughout the ages and
that there has come up out of the psychic, or subjective,
experience in every age a definite belief in obsessing
spirits. I don't believe in "obsessing spirits"; I don't think
it's possible. If it *were* possible, it's very easy to get rid
of them. One treatment will do it in any case I've ever
known—dissolved right there, just by knowing their
nothingness.

You couldn't exorcise or cast out a devil, you couldn't
separate a discarnate spirit from an incarnate personality, if the spirit were an entity. It doesn't make any sense;
and because of that, I've never believed that apparent

spirit obsessions *were* spirit obsessions. I know enough about it to know that they act like it, and look like it, and that they can, apparently, take temporary physical form and talk like it—but I don't believe they *are* it at all. They are merely something that comes up out of some psychic power that we have *within ourselves* that we don't know enough about yet to use consciously and definitely as we do other things.

I have no thought of criticism of anyone who believes in discarnate spirits, but I do not believe it's always the way it seems to be. If a person *were* obsessed by a spirit, that would only mean he had invited that spirit or uses it. But if you can dissolve, by your thinking, whatever that is, you are dissolving a *thought-form*. You might be dissolving a memory image attached to that person. You might be dissolving a thought-form that is created out of the person's unconscious, or the unconscious of people around him. But you certainly would not be casting out a dynamic entity with choice and volition and will. If we were to go so far as to say it was a detached *personification* of a personality, but not a *personality*—in other words, the astral or more subtle form—we would still find that we were not dealing with *people*; we would be dealing with a psychic, a mental, or subjective phenomenon. I'm thoroughly convinced that is what it is.

I had this most interesting experience a number of years ago. A friend came to one of our lectures and later asked me to come out to her house. She said, "Now, we have 'friends' who will come in."* I've always been fascinated by this kind of thing; it never has seemed weird or

*I.e., spirit visitants.

unnatural or uncanny. Always it has seemed to me to be part of what *is*, like snowflakes or grains of sand. I think we should deny nothing, affirm nothing that we don't understand, accept nothing that seems irrational, but always keep our minds open to be convinced, never against our will but by the logic of events. Always reserve the prerogative of choosing what you think, but never be unwilling to accept the testimony of evidence.

One of the great mistakes that supposedly scientific investigators in the psychic field make is the skepticism with which they enter the séance room. Their skepticism prohibits the phenomena they hope to experience. These things only happen when the psychic atmosphere is right. That follows its own law. I have said to these skeptical investigators, "It's unscientific to deny the possibility of any principle, just because you don't know about it. It's unscientific to deny these conditions, to refuse to subject yourselves to the conditions necessary."

Any number of times I have seen completely independent writing. In automatic writing, the force controls your own arm. I can do that; anyone can, if they really try—not that there's any value in doing it. Then there is the completely independent writing, where no one touches the pencil, where there is no physical contact. There is an apparent, intelligent direction which seems to be confined to a very limited field.

The Unobstructed Universe, by Stewart Edward White, is one of the best books I've read in this field. It's really a very wonderful book. It is the only one that carries on much intelligent discussion of what happens and how it happens and of the nature of the physical universe.

I have seen an almost illiterate person who was told

that he was connected up with the spirit of Socrates or Plato write one of the most profoundly philosophical articles that could be written—an article which, in his normal state, he couldn't even understand. I don't think Plato or Socrates was there. I believe that the person contacted the stream of consciousness. I think we do that as we read between the lines of the great poets and the great essayists. I read Emerson's essays several times a year, and I never read them without getting a new insight into Emerson. Now, I don't think Emerson is there, although many times when I've been studying Emerson or Whitman, psychics have told me that they *are* there and have described them. That looks like a memory image, doesn't it?

I always wondered about Jesus walking over the water until I saw levitation. Levitation means that a physical object, an object with weight, is lifted without any physical contact. I have seen people lifted out of their chairs and suspended in the air and put down in another chair. That's levitation—the thing that many think can be done only by people with terrific spiritual concentration. The funny thing about it is that it has nothing to do with spiritual concentration. Some people can do it and some cannot. That's all we know about it. Some people can develop so that they can do it; apparently others cannot.

The levitation Dr. von Koerber saw in a lamasery in Tibet had nothing to do with spiritual evolution. Those people are no more evolved spiritually than we are—just in a different way. That's my opinion. I think we are the most evolved nation the world has ever known. There is no evidence that there ever was a greater one.

When I saw levitation for the first time, I said, "Well,

that's the way Jesus walked over the water." He didn't walk *on* it. He came through the air—I don't know how; but it's a law, and it's in the realm of reality. When, for the first time, I saw things pass through walls, I said, "That's the way Jesus appeared in their midst." There they were in the upper chamber, and suddenly Jesus was there. *He knew how to do it.* He probably knew how to do it consciously and definitely, and it helps us to better understand what he was able to do. It does not tell us *how* he did it, nor is there any evidence so far that there is anyone who knows exactly how it is done or that anyone can transmit that power, whatever it is.

Eileen Garrett came to me a number of years ago. You all know who she is: she's the world's most famous medium, I presume. She's the one they did so much experimentation with at Duke University. She is a very scientific person. She told me Dr. Brown at the University of London said that if she would subject herself to a complete analysis, he would dissolve her alleged control.* She answered, "I'd like to do it for the scientific value, but I'm afraid to do it because I don't want to lose my clairvoyance."

I said, "Eileen, if your control is merely a subconscious split—a multiple or dual personality, psychologically— and he† reintegrates your mind psychically, then that control will disappear, because he‡ was never there. It is *you* impersonating the thing. Your clairvoyance he could

*A personality or spirit believed to direct the actions of a spiritualist medium.
†I.e., Dr. Brown.
‡I.e., the control.

no more analyze out of you than he could analyze your fingernails off. What is, can't be changed. You can only change the way you use it."

At any rate, he worked with her for a year and a half and at the end of that time he said, "I'm not getting anywhere. I've never met with such resistance"—not from her, but from her control. "I wish," he told her, "that you'd go into just one more trance; then we'll quit." So she went into another trance and he talked with her control. He asked, "Why haven't I been able to get rid of you?" and the reply was, "We don't enter by the same door. I come in one door, and you through another." An interesting remark.

And there was the famous case of Katy King. Sir William Crookes* was examining and working with a medium by the name of Home, or Hume, or some such name. He began to investigate to show up a fraud and instead became one of the early and most enthusiastic advocates; but like all the men who belong to the American and British academic societies, he discredited ninetenths of all evidence because of the interpretation given it. They didn't deny the phenomena, because they couldn't.

This woman, Katy King, came to them† over a period of years and she would remain for hours. They even cut off pieces of cloth from her garment and if she came back with the same garment there would seem to be a hole in it where they had cut out the piece. They took pictures, they weighed her, they talked with her.

*(1832–1919), British chemist and physicist, discoverer of the element thallium and inventor of the first cathode ray tube (CRT).
†I.e., as an apparition, immaterially.

Dr. Crookes examined her for heartbeat and respiration. They found everything a normal person would have physically—digestive organs and everything working—yet she would appear out of nothing and then disappear. This went on for several years. Then she told them, "I won't be coming very much any more." And finally she didn't come any more at all.

This is one of the most famous cases, attested to by probably 20 eminent scientists in England and hundreds of other people. There isn't any question about its validity. The question is merely *what is it*? People in our field have no right to be ignorant about psychic or philosophical things, religious or psychological things. Insofar as we know enough about them to put the whole works together, to create a vast synthesis out of all the different fields that so many people have analyzed, we must try to find a common meeting ground or an adequate medium through which all of these things take place, one that's sane and intelligent, not weird—because so much that has taken place in the psychic field is just that.

I want to show you what Rhine discovered. He discovered that telepathy is a principle in Nature. He announced two years ago that there is no thought transference—nothing has to go anywhere: *it's already there*. The same thing happens in what we call psychometry. When a medium, or a psychic or subjective person, takes a ring that belongs to someone who has passed on, they psychometrize it, and through this they enter the subjective atmosphere of the person who wore it. This is the key, the psychic or subjective vibration that was attached to that person. Maybe it still is, I don't know. But from that they can tell the whole past of that person, and, just as when a person is hypnotized, they can go back into their memory, sometimes even before birth. Dr. Phillips told me that he has traced traumatic shock a number of times to prenatal conditions.

"As above, so beneath; as below, so above." What's true on one plane is true on all. All the laws of nature are reproduced on the varying planes in exactly the same way, but in a way that belongs to the plane on which it is reproduced. As the Bible says, there are bodies celestial and bodies terrestrial. The "halls of Time" (let's say, the subjective mind of the world) are a world memory, a world subjective mind which is the repository for the whole collective experience of the human race. It is my belief that in this world memory are built up all the great negations of the human race: the doubts, the fears, the superstitions, the misunderstandings, the hatreds, the ugliness—as well as the loves and the beauty. All these things exist in our own individual psyche, and as we contact the world, the world vibrates to one or another particular thing. If we are clairvoyant, we see it; if clairaudient, we hear it; or, if only impressionistic, we feel it.

For instance, several years ago, certain people got together in Santa Ana to talk about something that was some of my business. I was suddenly aware that they were there, I knew who they were, and I knew what they were saying. Two of them had come from the East. They weren't mean people by any means, but they were doing something that really was my business and that I should have known about. That's why I tuned in on it. I've deliberately stopped doing that kind of thing because it is disturbing . . . everyone isn't always thinking happily about you, you know!

The idea is this: there is only one Subjective Mind in the Universe. That's all. Each one of us has his center in it. There is a way in which if a person listens to his own mind, he can listen to anything that was ever said in the world, by anyone; but he would have to tune into it. Fortunately, we don't do it. Consider the sum total of the effect and the result, and what we know about thought patterns, and see the resistance that comes to the thought *"There doesn't have to be another war."* All the smart boys in the world say, "There has *always* been war. There always will be." But there doesn't have to be! If that subjective thing that impinges on the minds of the whole race were excised, you'd never have another war.

I have probably known more mediums than most people know, and more good ones. I imagine there are many quacks among the mediums, but I have never met one—not *one*. They're as honest as any people I've ever known. I don't think it's possible for a medium in a trance to be dishonest, because they are no longer using their intellect. Their subjective patterns are coming to the surface—and when they get through, they don't know what they've said or done. I don't mean by that that I would accept everything they say, or their interpretation of it, because I think it's just like prayer. We know how prayers are answered, now, pretty well. We don't have to resort to superstition about it.

Let us consider the prophetic vision. The best book on the subject is Dunne's* *Experiment with Time*. He discovered that he was dreaming things that would happen—for example, Hiroshima two years before the atomic

*John William Dunne (1875-1949), British airplane designer and philosopher.

bomb fell. A strange thing happened to *me* one day. I was sitting down in my office giving a treatment, and all at once I seemed to be sitting on the side of a hill. I knew I was looking over a city. I knew it was Japan. I didn't know *where* in Japan, but I knew it was Japan. Then I saw something happen like a white cloud and something said, "That's a bomb!" I looked again, and there wasn't any city there. For several days I was nauseated. I said to myself, "Lord, it has been bombed! This is not destruction: it's annihilation!"*

That noon, Reginald Armor† and a couple of other people had lunch with me. I said, "I want to tell you something. I don't know when it's going to happen, but the war with Japan will end suddenly, because we have a bomb." This was before the *scientists* knew what was going to happen!‡ *I knew they were working on a bomb, different from anything that ever was*. I didn't know *what* it was; but I knew, when it exploded, that everything was dust. I knew they would try it over Japan and that it would annihilate a city and end the war—and that it was the most abominable thing that ever happened in the history of the human race: because we're not ready for it. They said, "That's crazy." I said, "All right. I will draw it and explain to you what it looks like. It's not imagination; that's the way it *is*."

---

*See *Seminar Lectures* (Holmes), p. 105.
†Reginald C. Armor (1903–1977), an early associate of Dr. Holmes.
‡The feasibility of developing a nuclear bomb had become clear to physicists by the end of the 1930s. That this was true could not have been known to Dr. Holmes at the time, especially in the atmosphere of intense secrecy that surrounded this matter for many years.

Other things have come to me: an atomic bullet that will make land armies obsolete, an airplane out of sight up in the stratosphere that shoots a beam. You will see these things; you will see them happen. Where do these things come from? What a terrific thing it would be if we could consciously develop that part of ourselves and know! Like this thing of seeing that atomic bomb explode over there. I could tell you of several other experiences of a like nature; one in England and one on this continent. It was not terrifying, but one of the most wonderful and prophetically happy visions that anyone could possibly have. Don't ever think that everything won't be all right. You don't need to worry about our country, whether you're a Republican or a Democrat.

This is the way the spirit of prophecy works. Its whole field is the field of simultaneous unity and instantaneous deduction, arriving at a logical conclusion with no process of time, or thought, or effort. It's true; our own subconscious mind is that way. That's what we mean when we say it deduces only; it doesn't *induce*, it doesn't analyze. There *is* such a field of reality, and that part of our psyche which we call the subconscious is merely the place where we use the universal Principle. Therefore, any sequence set in motion contains from the outset every step in the process, everything that is going to happen. The Alpha and the Omega are the same thing. Anyone who is psychic or subjective contacts this at any point if it comes to the surface. He won't see any process; what he *will* see is *the completed thing*—because the entire potential is present in the beginning. The picture of it is in the beginning.

It sounds fatalistic, doesn't it? But it has nothing to do

with fate. Here is the difference between Karma and Kismet.* Karma is the seat of action, polarity—action and reaction. Kismet we do not believe in; Karma we have to accept—but not necessarily through a cycle of reincarnation.

Suppose we say there is a window, and a ball is about to go through the window at a mile a minute. The window is going to be broken by the ball going through it. Now suppose someone is standing there with a net. He'll catch the ball, and then the window won't be broken.† That's what we do when we give a treatment. We do not deny the logical sequence of the cause and effect.

This is an interesting subject and I've only barely touched it. I have seen things that seem pretty weird and experienced things that seem fantastic, yet I know they are in the realm of a mental field which some day we'll understand completely. The way I saw Hiroshima and the bomb was that way.

On another occasion, I saw something I was never able to verify. I told it to a man who was very pro-English, and after I told him, he said, "What will happen to England?" I said, "I don't know but I'll see if I can find out." One day I was successful in at least getting an impression. I seemed to be up in the air, looking down over England. The contour seemed all flat, but it was the shape of England, and great waves came. I watched very carefully to see if the waves ever went over the whole place. They

---

*"The Karmic Law is not Kismet. It is not fate but cause and effect" (SOM 30:4).
†See SOM 355:4. Chapter 21, "Some Phases of the Subjective Life," pp. 347–356, holds much of relevance to this talk.

never did, they came in and washed back. I said to myself, "England will never be invaded!" And then as I
looked, there were hundreds of big flat boats, filled with
soldiers in uniform, and I knew they were getting ready
to invade England. They came out of the water and there
seemed to be great flames of oil and fire which completely enveloped them. They jumped into the water, and
I would say I saw hundreds of people drowning and burn-
ing. I said, "They are going to try to invade England." It
never happened. Whether it might have happened, had
it gone on, I don't know. I was never able to verify it.*

Next week we're going to talk about illumination, or
spiritual enlightenment. Real illumination is the letting
down of the Cosmic reality to the point of our objective
mentality. This doesn't mean that the world of appearance is an illusion. The illusion is not in the thing, but in
our interpretation of it—always. We never deny a fact to
affirm a principle. We never deny a fact to establish a
faith.

Next week I want to explain who the illumined were,
what happened to them, and what they discovered.

*Germany planned just such an invasion—Operation Sea Lion—for
1940 but aborted it. A "top" military secret, it nevertheless became
known to Allied authorities through cryptanalysis but remained
unknown to the public—and so to Dr. Holmes.

6

<u>Wednesday 20 February 1952</u>

"NEWS FROM THE KINGDOM OF HEAVEN"
COSMIC CONSCIOUSNESS

A s someone has said, we know why we are here, but we do not know, or haven't discovered, why we are "not all there." That is the search that science and religion and philosophy are making: to find the missing link between the Infinite/Absolute and the finite/relative—between the Mind of God and the mind of man, or Cosmic action and human activity—by means of a law, inherent within God's own being, that creates. Someone asked me the meaning of the saying in our textbook "To him who can perfectly practice inaction, all things are possible."* It means that all action comes out of that which to our action seems inaction. As Emerson said, "We are begirt with spiritual laws."

The whole basis of spiritual science, of the philosophy of metaphysics and its practice, lies in the concept that the Universe is self-existent, self-energizing, self-propelling,

*SOM 289:3.

self-knowing, and self-acting—and that everything that is, takes place within one infinite Self which is undivided and indivisible, but which, out of its own unity, creates this vast multiplication of Itself, this great variation of life.

This is not difficult to understand, if we think of it as simple. Everything in Nature proves what we teach, but the implications of Nature are very seldom carried out to discover the meaning of what it proves and the relationship of the thing proven to that which proved it. Immanuel Kant* said that we are able to recognize an external object, or an *apparently* external object, because it awakens an intuition within us in a field that is simultaneous and instantaneous. Dr. Rhine discovered that when he proved the law of mental telepathy and then went on to say that nothing passes from one point to another. It is already at that point!

We have discussed the theory and practice of Religious Science, and last week we discussed the field of psychic phenomena, very inadequately. Tonight we will discuss what we call the field of Cosmic Consciousness, which provides a logical conclusion to this brief series of sketchy thoughts about things in which we are deeply interested— our relationship to Life, to God, the possibility of the human soul, the probability of eternal evolution, the realization of immortality now, and the concept that the Universe itself can hold nothing against any individual.

Tonight we want to talk about what a group of people have discovered—but not in the realm of physical, mental, or psychic science. The other day I received a

*(1724–1804), German philosopher.

record of Mahatma Gandhi's,* in which he briefly discusses the epitome of his philosophy. He says he must accept the teachings and the discoveries and the truths of the great men of spiritual attainment throughout the ages, of all religions and all groups, because they all bear witness, they all coincide, come to the same conclusion. It is from these people that we learn the great spiritual truths.

There are two interesting books with which you are perhaps familiar: Huxley's† *The Perennial Philosophy* and Cheney's‡ *Men Who Have Walked with God*. Still another is Bucke's§ *Cosmic Consciousness*. These books describe what we are talking about tonight.

I would like to begin with a discussion of what the great spiritual minds of the ages have believed. Only from the great minds have we learned what God is like. The only knowledge we have of the kingdom of heaven must come through the consciousness of man. Therefore, man's thought should swing between prayer and meditation and contemplation and action. There has never been a great system of thought which has not taught a trinity of Spirit —what we term mind, soul, body. When I wrote our textbook, I reduced it to its simplest common denominator because we are dealing with the great abstractions of the ages. The attempt was made to put it in a language that all can understand: The Thing, The Way It Works, and What It Does.

*Mohandas Gandhi (1869–1948), Indian nationalist leader.
†Aldous Huxley (1894–1963), English novelist and critic.
‡Sheldon Cheney (1886–1980), American critic.
§Richard Maurice Bucke (1837–1902), Canadian psychoanalyst.

Here we have the Spirit or the Absolute, and we have this medium, or the Law of Mind in action (the psychic world), and we have the body—manifestation, or effect. The divine spark falls, we will say, to the lowest arc of the material, to the lowest objective manifestation of the "mundane clod." In all sacred literature you read references to this. It is that spark which impregnates everything and is buried in everything. It is the spark which Browning said we can desecrate but never quite lose. It is always there, and it contains within itself the upward push of all evolution.

The evolutionary process that impels things upward and onward from lower to higher forms of intelligence is occasioned because everything is impregnated with intelligence as unconscious memory, not as an intellectual conception. The *logic* of Spirit is in the intellect, but the Spirit is in the heart. The logic of faith may be in the intellect as a mathematical equation; the Spirit is something that cannot be analyzed or dissected. You can kill the nightingale but you cannot capture its song. Here is the spark that causes all evolution.

Since everything is an individualization of the Universal, every spark is alike in that it is divine. It is made of the same Cosmic stuff, but no two sparks are identical. The process in Nature is the multiplication of an infinite variation of unified identities, no one of which is identical with the other, even though each and all are in the same field.

Unity and uniformity are not the same thing. No two blades of grass are alike. What does it mean, spiritually? It means that incarnated within each one of us is not only a divine Spark, not only an incarnation of the living Spirit of the Cosmos, but a unique presentation of the Cosmic Whole, if we can judge the Unknown by the known. We have nothing to disprove and everything to prove that this individualization of the Spirit in each one of us, rooted in common soil, having the characteristics and potentialities of its common background, contains what the ancients called the microcosm.

We have every reason to suppose that there is, back of and within and around every individual, the divine representation of himself as the Son of God, forever expanding. The Universe is alive and awake and aware. It's an interesting thing that all the great intuitions of the ages are gradually being verified by the investigations of modern science. The nature of the physical universe has been known intuitively from time immemorial; but that which anciently was conceived by the intuition, which went in the front door of the Spirit by a natural and logical affinity, is, in our day and generation, gradually being reproven by the inductive method of science, which goes in the back door of the Spirit, but which, when it gets into the living room, sees the same furniture.

Pythagoras declared that the physical universe is made up of a fluid which is the substance of all form, and that the only thing that determines the difference in the form and its identity is the rate of vibration of the original substance. Einstein said the same thing. The change takes place within the changeless. Time is a measure of experience in the timeless; space is an outline of that experience. Every "relative" is the Absolute at the level of its own relativity, containing the nature and the will and the purpose of the Infinite in that which appears to be finite merely because it must be outlined and circumscribed, or else the Absolute would never be expressed. It's important for us to understand this.

There is no such thing as a nonconscious Consciousness; there is no such thing as a Creator who doesn't create. That's why the Bible says, "World without end, amen." The moment you assume an infinite Creator, you've got to assume an infinite Creation. The moment you assume an infinite Consciousness, you've got to assume that there is something that the Consciousness is conscious of.

Therefore, the Spirit is the Power that knows itself. In knowing itself, it sees itself in everything it does: it beholds the manifestation. In our theology, it is said that God made man for his own glory and his own edification. The ancients said God creates everything for pure delight. I like that. You see, God is all there is—there isn't anything else, there's nothing to make anything else out of. Nothing. Therefore, God is in every manifestation. God is in all creation—but greater than his creation.

The lowest form of evolution will be that which has no conscious awareness whatever. There is Mind that sleeps in the mineral, waves in the vegetable, and wakes to simple consciousness in the animal, to self-consciousness in man, and to Cosmic Consciousness in an ever-ascending hierarchy of evolved beings. That is what the Bible means when it says we are surrounded by powers and witnesses. Jesus was telling the story of human evolution in the story of the Prodigal Son, the unfoldment of every individual. It's the greatest story ever told because it's Cosmic and human at the same time. We start with the very lowest form, but the Spirit never leaves it—there's a push, an urge, an emergence to do, to be; and through all of this it is still God.

Those of you who have read the Bhagavad Gita remember that it begins with a discussion between Krishna, Lord of Life, and Arjuna, the human. A great battle is going on in which many relatives are engaged, and Arjuna says, "I cannot go out and kill them." Krishna answers, "It's just a play of Life upon itself." In Edwin Arnold's beautiful translation:

> Never the spirit was born; the spirit
>   shall cease to be never;
> Never was time it was not; End and
>   Beginning are dreams!
> Birthless and deathless and change-
>   less remaineth the spirit forever;
> Death hath not touched it at all,
>   dead though the house of it seems!
>
> . . . .
>   . . . as when one layeth
> His worn-out robes away,
> And, taking new ones, sayeth,
>   "These shall I wear today!"
> So putteth by the spirit
>   Lightly its garb of flesh,
> And passeth to inherit
>   A residence afresh.

There is an intuition in man that knows he is immortal. Our modern science is proving it, but it is merely verifying, by an inductive method, something within us that has always known.

Evolution is the emergence of that which already is in form, in an ever-upward spiraling. "Ever as the spiral grew, / He left the old house for the new." Or, as Tennyson said:

> Our little systems have their day;
> They have their day and cease to be:
> They are but broken lights of Thee,
> And Thou, O Lord, art more than they.

Every great poet has said it, because the poet speaks from the intuition, from a Cosmic Soul. Every great poem is written by one writer, which is God, and differentiated to the point that it may bear witness to itself and the variation of its own words.

In ancient and occult literature and in all our esoteric books, there is reference to the tree, with its trunk in the ground, and to another tree up in the heavens with its branches down here. This is the Tree of Life.* The symbolism of the serpent and the Savior is contained in this imagery, because it was the serpent that became the Savior when it was elevated and the Life Principle was no longer viewed from the lowest arc of evolution, but from the highest. Jesus said, "As Moses lifted up the serpent in

---

*"The medieval Qabbalists represented creation as a tree with its roots in the reality of spirit and its branches in the illusion of tangible existence. The . . . tree was therefore inverted, with its roots in heaven and its branches upon the earth. . . . The Qabbalistic tree . . . is not only a macrocosmic symbol but also the emblem of man himself, for he, too, is rooted in spirit."—Manly P. Hall, *The Secret Teachings of all Ages* (Philosophical Research Society), p. xciv.

the wilderness, even so must the Son of Man be lifted up."

Here is the evolutionary benediction from heaven and the evolutionary impulsion from here. The two have to get together. What's the purpose of it? Why didn't God in his infinite wisdom do it differently? God didn't create people to go through hardships. There are certain things that even an infinite Intelligence cannot do, and one of them is it cannot create a spontaneous mechanism. That would contradict the nature of God. The necessity is what the ancients called "the great ignorance" and what our theology often misstates as the problem of evil. There is no problem of evil in the Universe; there is only a problem of ignorance. Emerson said, "Ignorance is the only sin, and enlightenment is the only salvation." Somebody else said, "There is no sin but a mistake, and no punishment but a consequence." It's right.

The individual must emerge and, as it does so, it has to be let alone to make all the discoveries for itself, because when it returns to its Father's house, it must come back an individualization of the Infinite. It must know itself. It must know its environment, because salvation is not the loss of identity. As Tagore* said, "Nirvana is not absorption but immersion, as an arrow is lost in its mark." In other words, we are not to be *lost* in God, but *found* in God. There is a great difference. The identity is never to become extinguished or obliterated—merely increased eternally. There will never be a place where you stop. Never.

*Rabindranath Tagore (1861–1941), Indian poet.

What has happened in the process of evolution? This great conclusion of the ages—the most far-reaching, the most sweeping, the most fascinating and intriguing conclusion the human mind has ever come to—is what Browning called man: "A God though in the germ." He writes:

> . . . Praise be thine!
> I see the whole design,
> I, who saw power, see now Love perfect
> too:
> Perfect I call thy plan:
> Thanks that I was a man!
> Maker, remake, complete—I trust what thou
> shalt do!
> . . . .
> Therefore, I summon age
> To grant youth's heritage,
> Life's struggle having so far reached
> its term;
> Thence shall I pass, approved
> A man, for aye removed
> From the developed brute; a God though
> in the germ.*

Let us say it starts here—with atomic intelligence. It doesn't know it's intelligent. It has no consciousness; but the spark is there. It gradually awakes a little in simple consciousness in the animal kingdom. It passes from there to the human being where there is, in evolution, an inner

*From "Rabbi Ben Ezra."

awareness which gradually formulates it into individualization. Remember, the whole purpose is for every spark to expand to infinity but remain the individual spark—never less, but always more. Emerson in *The Natural History of the Intellect,* in his chapter "The Laws of Thought," says that he awaits the advent of a person who can liken all the laws of nature to the laws of thought. We're gradually doing that. The next step is the awakening of the human to the Divine. That is what all the great spiritual leaders have talked and written about. It is the whole meaning of Whitman's* *Leaves of Grass* and of Carpenter's† "Towards Democracy."

We have, now, in our physical and in our mental being, all of these lower forms of intelligence gradually building up to a higher form. There's always a body somewhere, because there is a body within a body to infinity. There are "bodies celestial and bodies terrestrial." Each step is a broader awareness, a higher altitude. The clod down here has an impulsion to roll uphill, and in the process it looks up; and it sees something more, it becomes something more.

All through the Bible there is mention of the sea. It says that God moved upon the face of the deep. Moses was found in a little ark floating on the sea—which means the Life principle. Jonah fell into the sea and was swallowed by a whale, or "a great fish," and cast up on dry land. The fish stands for the Christ Consciousness or Principle. That's why the early Christians used the sign of the fish as a symbol. Revelation says that when final redemption

---

*Walt Whitman (1819–1892), American poet.
†Edward Carpenter (1844–1929), English writer.

comes for man, there shall be no more sea. You wouldn't find this illustration going through this esoteric book, from beginning to end, unless it had a profound spiritual significance in the evolution of the human race. The story of the Bible is the story of the evolution of the human race and the emancipation of that spark which is caught in the first mundane clod, impregnating it with the will to drive onward and upward.

The *psychic sea* means the sum total of all human thought, all human confusion. The Bible calls it the carnal mind. Mrs. Eddy calls it mortal mind. The sum total of the thoughts of the ages, based on a sense of duality, has created not a psychic *opposition to* good, but a psychic *contradiction of* it. Nothing opposes good, though much seems to contradict it. There is no final power of evil, even if the individual life builds up a subjective reaction which contradicts its good, denies our wholeness, our happiness, our freedom, and builds a barrier against that which we feel we ought to be. Wordsworth described it when he wrote of the child coming from heaven. Gradually as the "prison" walls close around him, he forgets that celestial palace whence he came:

> Our birth is but a sleep and a forgetting;
> The Soul that rises with us, our life's Star,
>   Hath had elsewhere its setting
>   And cometh from afar:
>   Not in entire forgetfulness,
>   And not in utter nakedness,
> But trailing clouds of glory do we come
>   From God who is our home:
> Heaven lies about us in our infancy!

Shades of the prison-house begin to close
    Upon the growing Boy
But He beholds the light, and whence it flows,
    He sees it in his joy;
The Youth, who daily farther from the east
    Must travel, still is Nature's Priest,
    And by the vision splendid
    Is on his way attended;
At length the Man perceives it die away,
And fade into the light of common day.*

What we now know is the reaction of our subconscious or subjective self, which is not another mind, but a field of mentation surrounding us. Such a field of thought envelops the whole planet—mortal mind, carnal mind, collective unconscious, race belief, the barrier that keeps us imprisoned in the lower state. This is called the problem of good and evil, but the ancients merely called it "the great ignorance." I like that; it makes sense. It isn't a problem. It isn't a thing in itself. It isn't even a law unto itself, because it exists only as a phantom, detached. What is it that says, "You can't have honest people in public office. Everybody is corrupt"? It's not God talking. It's ignorance talking. It isn't even *evil* talking, because evil of itself is neither person, place, nor thing. It's just a state of consciousness. It's *nothing* claiming to be *something*—but it's more than nothing, because it builds up this terrific barrier. The Bible says there shall be no more sea because the earth shall be filled with the knowledge of God as the waters fill the ocean.

*From "Intimations of Immortality."

There are those in India who practice, first, the control of the physical body, observing the practices of Yoga. But we in the Western world have another way. We are beneficiaries of the Divine, but also, as Emerson says, recipients of human ignorance; and probably we are hypnotized from the cradle to the grave—ninety percent. Emerson says that once in a while somebody wakes up and looks around, and, although he sinks back into the stupor, he is never the same afterward. Never. We should seek to liberate the consciousness that is so hypnotized by conditions.

In *Cosmic Consciousness*, Bucke gives an account of about 60 people who have received illumination and shows that each one of them discovered the same thing. We might take just one of the 60 smartest people you could find in the United States and say to him: "It has been proven that on the other side of these mountains there is a beautiful valley. We don't know anything about it. Will you go there, stay for a while, and come back and tell us what you found?" All right, he goes. He comes back and says, "This is what I found: everything very wonderful." We might do the same with the rest of the 60, one at a time. Each one has had to make the journey alone.

The discovery these people made would be a self-discovery. They may have seen slightly different sights, different kinds of life, music, sunsets, etc. But when the evidence is all in, each report is separate from the other only in minutest detail. Everyone who has penetrated the psychic veil brings back a logic that is irresistible, and there's an intuition in all of us which follows it and knows it's true. These people just got a little nearer to the Maker of all music, to the Master of all singing.

It is destined that good shall come at last to all alike. Nothing is more certain than what we call the salvation of the individual soul. Religion is our feeling of God by intuition. It descends from the higher to the lower levels, to get down into our intellects, which are encased and encrusted beneath great ignorance. It does get through, however, because we all have intuition.

John said, "Beloved, now are we the sons of God, and its does not yet appear what we shall be. But we know that when He shall appear, we shall be like Him; for we shall see Him as He is." Beloved, now are we the sons of God: we don't know what we shall become, because we haven't yet evolved into what we are going to be. But when He shall appear, we shall see that we are like Him; and He will appear when we shall see Him as He is. That's something, isn't it?

I was talking with Adela Rogers St. Johns* this morning over the telephone, and I promised to give a talk on "Spiritual Democracy," or the spiritual obligation we owe our government. In the course of our talk I said: "You know, Adela, I think religion itself is an intuition which the mind has, because it's never entirely separated from its source. It only seems to be. But when this intuition breaks into the background of our experience and the world experience and gets down to where it hits the intellect, it becomes changed and modified until, finally, the intuition suffers the shock of all human experience and

*(1894–1988), American journalist and author.

becomes theology." We interpret or misinterpret the original impressions. That's why Jesus said, "Become as little
children. . . . for I say unto you, that in heaven their
angels do always behold the face of my Father which is
in heaven." Look on the Deity, and the Deity will look
on thee.

The whole process of evolution was necessary for the
emergence of Cosmic individualization, that every man
might be on the pathway of his own life; that every man,
whether he knew it or not, might set the law of his life;
for there is no law other than the law that he sets—as it
comes into conjunction with the one universal Law of
Cause and Effect. He cannot change the Law, but the very
power which limits and binds him, rightly used, can free
him. There is nothing between us and God but our own
thoughts and beliefs.

Hush, hush; 'tis thine own self that hinders thee.
'Tis thine own thoughts that bother thee.

Jesus defined these things in a way that an unlettered
multitude could understand. He said: God is your Father.
God is within you and around you. God knows what you
have need of. Act as though God will respond, and believe that He will respond; but don't judge according to
appearances. Don't judge according to tradition.

Jesus found himself on the other side of the wall that
separates heaven from earth. He knew that heaven is lost
merely for the lack of an idea of harmony, and that hell
is peopled with the phantoms of our own tragic fears and
doubts.

There is a necessity for accepting the testimony of the wise and illumined of the ages. They have actually brought news from the kingdom of heaven. Our whole endeavor here is not to convince people that they are great or wise or small.

What I have contributed to this movement (and it is very little personally) is to "liken the laws of Nature to the laws of thought," and

. . . judging God by what is best in man,
With a child's trust, lean on a Father's breast.

Science of Mind:
It Will Change Your Life

Recognized as one of the foremost spiritual teachers of this century, Ernest Holmes blended the best of Eastern and Western spiritual philosophies, psychology, and science into the transformational ideas known as the Science of Mind. Additionally, he formulated a specific type of meditative prayer, known as Spiritual Mind Treatment, that has positively changed the lives of millions.

Basing his techniques for living a free and full life on sacred wisdom, from the ancient to the modern, Ernest Holmes outlines these ideas in a collection of inspiring books. Written with simplicity and clarity, these books provide the means for every reader to live a more satisfying life.

For a list of books by Ernest Holmes, call 1-800-382-6121.

Visit **Science of Mind** online
http://www.scienceofmind.com

The award-winning *Science of Mind* magazine presents insightful and uplifting articles, interviews, and features each month. Additionally, the magazine's *Daily Guides to Richer Living* provides you with spiritual wisdom and guidance every day of the year.

For more information, call 1-800-247-6463.